The Beautiful Disappointment

COLIN McCARTNEY

THE

Beautiful

DISAPPOINTMENT

DISCOVERING WHO YOU ARE THROUGH THE TRIALS OF LIFE

FOREWORD BY TONY CAMPOLO

The Beautiful Disappointment:
Discovering Who You Are Through the Trials of Life

Published by:
Castle Quay Books
1-1295 Wharf Street, Pickering, Ontario, L1W 1A2
Tel: (416) 573-3249   Fax: (416) 981-7922
E-mail: info@castlequaybooks.com
www.castlequaybooks.com

Copy editing by Janet Diamond
Cover photo by Jimmie Hepp of JIMMIE4ART
Cover design by Essence Publishing
Printed at Essence Publishing, Belleville, Ontario

Library and Archives Canada Cataloguing in Publication

McCartney, Colin, 1964-

The beautiful disappointment : discovering who you are through the trials of life / Colin McCartney.

ISBN 978-1-894860-35-2

1. McCartney, Colin, 1964- 2. Life change events--Religious aspects--Christianity. 3. Self-perception--Religious aspects--Christianity.
4. Spirituality. 5. Christian life. I. Title.

BV4509.5.M3435 2007   248.4   C2007-905205-3

CASTLE QUAY BOOKS

TABLE OF CONTENTS

◆

ACKNOWLEDGEMENTS

◆

My life would never be as joyful and wonderful as it is without my beautiful wife Judith. She is God's best gift to me. He has made us one and I am so glad to be one with you.

To my children, C.J. and Victoria. You are my delight and joy. I am a very blessed father to have children like you. The future is yours—go God's way.

To my publisher, Larry Willard, and my editor, Janet Diamond, and Castle Quay Books. Thank you so much for your gracious touch that is felt in every page of this book.

I also want to personally acknowledge all of my family and friends who were there for us in our time of crisis. Thank you. To my UrbanPromise family, what a journey we live. I also want to say a very warm *aloha* to the wonderful friends, doctors, specialists and nurses we met at Maui Memorial Hospital, who were so wonderful to our family. We will always be grateful for the wonderful care we received. *Mahola*.

To the families in UrbanPromise who were affected deeply by the tragedies in this book and to all of us who will face more trials in the future. Jesus walks with us!

Finally, but most importantly, to my heavenly Father who is always present with exceeding amounts of comfort and grace. Life would be empty without You.

---◆---

"We can rest contentedly in our sins and in our stupidities, and everyone who has watched gluttons shoveling down the most exquisite foods as if they did not know what they were eating, will admit that we can ignore even pleasure. But pain insists upon being attended to. God whispers to us in our pleasures, speaks in our consciences, but shouts in our pains. It is his megaphone to rouse a deaf world."

– C. S. Lewis,
The Problem of Pain

INTRODUCTION

◆

In our lifetime, we will all experience an assortment of trials, both large and small. At times, come to us mysteriously, quietly dropping with a whisper into our subconscious. At others, they confront us with a loud scream. Often they invade our minds through the radio while driving to work. Or they can take on profound personal significance in a variety of shapes and sizes:

- A phone call informing you that a beloved family member is ill.
- Your boss telling you that your services are no longer needed.
- A letter outlining why you were not accepted into that college at which you were hoping to study.
- Your doctor's voice suggesting that surgery is needed immediately.
- Your spouse telling you that it is over.
- Your teenaged child's behaviour, changed from a pleasant presence into a bitter and depressed person whom you do not recognize.

This list can go on and on, testifying to the unavoidable reality that trials and tribulations are here to stay. We have all faced them. Many are dealing with them right now. We can all expect them in the future. Life truly is a struggle.

As I get older, I find that I am forced to deal with more and more trials. It seems that I am increasingly shaped by the struggles I face. However, as I stumble through life, tripping over many obstacles and making far too many mistakes, I have discovered a wonderful and comforting secret. I am beginning to understand that these trials are opportunities for personal growth. Though I am no longer a child, I now realize that I never stop growing as an adult, and the main instrument God uses to shape my being are His tools of trials and tribulations. My problems, in the hands of God, are mighty instruments He can use to refine me into becoming progressively more what He created me to be. I have discovered the truth of James' words when he wrote:

> "Consider it a sheer gift, friends, when tests and challenges come at you from all sides. You know that under pressure, your faith-life is forced into the open and shows its true colors. So don't try to get out of anything prematurely. Let it do its work so you become mature and well-developed, not deficient in any way." (James 1:2-4, The Message)

God is at work in me, freeing me to be all that He created me to be. The same can be said for you. This is why we can take comfort in knowing that every trial and tribulation we face opens the door to the possibility of being released from all the encumbrances and dross that has prevented us from becoming the incredible people God already sees us to be. He has created us with immense value, purpose and ability. However, the reason the "real us" hasn't been loosed is because we have imprisoned this true self in a hard shell of pride, weakness, selfishness and fear. Through life's struggles, God slowly chips away at these prison bars. Tribulations can become His hammer that breaks the chains and bars we have erected, keeping our very souls in captivity.

This book is about discovering the real you through the trials of life. As you read it, it is important to know that it is based on truths experienced in the fiery furnace of life. It is a challenge for you to accept the inevitability of suffering and to allow it to shape who you truly are deep within your soul. Though this book documents my real-life tragedies, it is an encouragement and demonstration of the love of God as evidenced in how He is involved in shaping our lives. We are not yet a finished product. Far from it. However, we are getting closer to completion because of the trials that we experience.

Great wisdom is often birthed from tragedy. It seems that God allows us to learn His most precious truths only from the depths of our own personal despair. In these pages, I share insights that I discovered during the darkest period of my life in which my family and I faced three seemingly insurmountable tragedies within nine months. The timeline of this book begins with the first two tragedies, and ends with the catastrophe that took place when we were on a sabbatical in Hawaii. It was in a state of complete physical, emotional and spiritual brokenness that I was able to invite God into my situation and into my year of heartbreak. From this vantage point, I was able to reflect on the past and was forced to meet with God in solitude. It was there that God impacted my life like never before.

It is in the eye of the storm, in the midst of disappointment, that you can experience the beauty of God who turns trials into gold. These times are what I call "beautiful disappointments," where God reveals Himself to us in powerful, life-changing ways! My prayer for you while you read this book is that it will encourage you to never give up and to embrace your circumstances. God has wonderful plans for you—if you let Him lead and comfort.

– Rev. Colin McCartney

FOREWORD

◆

By Tony Campolo

In the face of tragedy, you can always count on some well-meaning Christian quoting Romans 8:28, trying to remind you that "all things work together for good to those who trust God and are called according to His purposes." Sometimes, in quoting the verse, they add their un-theological interpretation, which goes something like this: "God is in control. Everything that happens is God's will!" I am not so sure about that these days. I have seen too many things happen to good people that did not turn out to be good at all. Maybe it's my lack of faith, and maybe someday in the future—perhaps in another life—I will understand the good that is inherent in the tragedies that I have seen.

In reality, I believe that the verse, if properly translated, would probably read something like this:

"In the midst of all the things that are happening, God is there at work and through it all will bring about His good."

That particular translation does not suggest that God makes everything happen. As a matter of fact, I am fairly convinced that God doesn't make everything happen. There is a lot of evil in this world, and God is not the author of evil. The Bible says so. He is not the author of tragedy. As a matter of fact, He is the one who only comes with blessings.

What the verse properly translated suggests is that no matter what happens—good or bad—people of faith know that God is with them in

13

the midst of their tragedies and He will work along with them to create some good. As a matter of fact, the good that He creates far exceeds our most optimistic imaginations.

As you read through this book, you will become acquainted with my friend Colin McCartney. He is a man who has committed his life to doing good for God and serving as a missionary in a very difficult inner-city situation. He and his wife are a couple of the most attractive people you could ever meet. Their photographs could easily be on the cover of a "health and happiness" magazine. They have beautiful children and seem to have everything that life could offer.

All of a sudden, tragedies struck Colin's life. Blow after blow landed upon him, and as you read this story, you will wonder how he ever survived the ordeals that occurred in such a short period of time and how he did so with his faith in God intact.

One time, when Mother Teresa was asked about the tragedies of life and how a loving God could allow such tragedies, her only response was, "When I see Him, He's got a lot of explaining to do!" Whenever I tell that story in a talk or in a sermon, I always humorously add, "That's probably why she lived so long. I can just hear God saying to the angel Gabriel, 'Don't bring her up here right now. I've got too much on my hands right now. I don't think I could handle her. Could you put off bringing her to me for just a little while?'"

In the face of the events that you are about to read about, you may be apt to ask, "Why did a loving God allow so much tragedy to enter into the life of a young man who was trying to do missionary work and serve some of the most poor and oppressed people in this country?"

This book is not, in any way, an attempt to answer that kind of question. Instead, it is a straightforward account of how a young missionary found the strength in God that enabled him to overcome the tragedies that befell him and his family and, not only to overcome, but to ascertain the good that God was doing in the midst of all that was happening.

I am not sure just how much God controls all the events of our lives, but reading through this book, I was convinced that in the midst of all that was happening to Colin McCartney, God was present and made some things happen that would be otherwise extremely unlikely. Colin McCartney is with us today, serving Christ in Toronto, Canada, because in the midst of the tragedies of his life, he became more aware than ever that God is a very present help in trouble; a strength in a time of weakness; and a source of hope in the face of despairing circumstances.

Colin's story starts with a description of some of the work that he and some heroic young people who work with him are doing in government housing communities in a giant metropolitan area. The story begins with the tragic and senseless murder of a young man named Patrick. This young man had been won to Christ through the efforts of Colin's ministry and had become a beacon of hope to boys and girls throughout the depressing neighborhood that had the deceptive name of Warden Woods. The name of this government housing community creates an image of a bucolic setting when in reality just the opposite is true. It's a community that is marked by gangs, juvenile delinquency, drugs, illicit sex and all the other maladies that mark so many of these kinds of neighbourhoods. There came to this neighbourhood the good news of a ministry that was developed under the direction of Colin McCartney, called UrbanPromise, which made an incredible impact on the people who lived there. Because of his work and his partnership with a friendly social worker, life had become better in Warden Woods and the murders, which had once been all too common, had seemingly come to an end. Then Patrick's murder broke the peace that UrbanPromise had helped to create. The loss of Patrick was a horrendous blow to Colin, his workers and especially to the boys and girls who looked up to Patrick as a symbol and sign that even kids growing up in desperate neighbourhoods could become wonderful people. In this book, you will see how Colin and his colleagues allowed God to permeate their lives in the midst of the suffering associated with this death and brought about incredible good.

Shakespeare once said, "When troubles come, they come not as single spies, but in battalions!" The truth of that quote was verified in Colin's life, because it wasn't too long after Patrick's murder that other tragedies confronted him.

Working as they do in inner-city settings, Colin and his co-workers with UrbanPromise try to run a variety of programs that not only lead children and teenagers to Christ, but also enable them to have the fun and cultural enrichment that children deserve and seldom enjoy.

One summer afternoon, some of the workers took a group of boys and girls to a lakeside beach near Toronto where they could have an outing under the sun and in the water. Again, tragedy struck. A little boy was accidentally drowned.

It wasn't that the workers were negligent. In reality, they were paying close attention and yet somehow this little boy ended up face-down in shallow water, and before anyone could rescue him he was in serious condition. It wasn't too long after that that the boy passed away in the hospital. Colin and company had been constantly at the bedside of the child, praying and asking God for healing, but healing didn't happen.

It was expected that the parents of the child would be full of anger and would lash out at the young workers of UrbanPromise. It didn't happen. The parents, who had been touched by the ministries of Colin over the past several years, demonstrated a love and sensitivity that to some outsiders might seem unthinkable. Their attitudes, their dispositions, their willingness to endure the loss of their little boy with spiritual serenity proved to be a testimony of how God could equip people to handle the extremely difficult circumstances of life.

The problems of Colin McCartney and UrbanPromise did not end after the two tragedies that I have cited above. Colin's friends knew that he needed a break, so a sabbatical was arranged. Some good people made a resort cottage in one of the most exclusive places in Hawaii available to Colin's family for an extended vacation, free of charge. From there, they were to go on to Australia and enjoy even more relaxation. But the McCartney family was soon to learn that the best-laid plans of men and women can often go awry. On the first day of surfing at a beach on the island of Maui, there was an accident and Colin McCartney was rendered paralyzed. As the book will clearly point out, there were scores of reasons why he should have died, but by an incredible array of circumstances he was rescued and over an extended period was restored to health and wellbeing.

When I heard about Colin's accident, I repeated to myself what Mother Teresa once said, "God! You'd have a lot more friends if you treated the few you have a little better." I was convinced that this would be the last straw, that Colin would never come back to ministry, and that he probably would end up being a bitter and disillusioned Christian. Just the opposite happened.

In this book, you will see how, in the midst of these circumstances, God did wonderful things for Colin and for his family. This book is the story of how, in enduring pain and facing death, Colin was able to reevaluate his priorities and come to an incredible awareness of the abiding presence of Christ. This is the story of how he learned through the circumstances of tragedy to slow down, reflect on life, pay renewed attention to his family and to reorder his values.

UrbanPromise is a fantastic ministry. The good news of this book is that this ministry is going to be stronger and more effective than ever before because of what God has brought out of the tragedies described in the pages that follow.

This is an inspiring book, but it is also a teaching book. It teaches us to be aware that on the other side of darkness there is God and on the other side of the silence of God there is a soft, still voice that gives assurance, not in words, but in the feeling that God is always there for us and that we must learn to trust Him in the midst of everything that goes on in our lives.

Tony Campolo, PhD
Eastern University

---◆---

"To the hustlas, killers, murderers, drug dealers even the strippers. Jesus walks with them. To the victims of welfare for we living in hell here hell yeah. Jesus walks with them."

– Kanye West, "Jesus Walks,"
from the album *The College Dropout,*
Roc-a-Fella Records (USA), 2004

MURDER IN THE CITY

◆

CHAPTER ONE

Tragedies are like earthquakes, unexpectedly striking with devastating consequences, overwhelming everything in their path. Though earthquakes are painful and destructive, there is one positive thing that can come out of the rubble—the opportunity to build anew from the ground up. Looking back over my life, there were many tremors, leaving cracks in my inner world that were unseen by others and ignored by me. On March 4, 2004, those cracks were torn open.

From that point on, things began to come crashing down around me. My busy, active and out-of-control life had to be shaken up before it could be rebuilt from the inner foundation of my soul. Before transformation can begin, destruction must occur. In my case, things started to fall apart on a cool March afternoon. Up to that point in my life, everything was going well—no problems, all sunshine and no clouds. However, within seconds, my world was turned into a tempest of tears, fear and confusion.

A call came from Nicola Lunn, my children's supervisor, who worked in an increasingly troubled urban community known as Scarborough in the city of Toronto. When I answered the phone and heard the intense tone of her voice, the crying and shortness of breath, I knew something bad had happened—but I had no idea how horrific. This was not a typical phone call from a staff person telling me that our passenger van was acting up or that their community petty cash fund had run out of money once again. This was much more serious. The voice was choppy, broken, sounding out of breath.

"I was just told that Patrick has been shot!"

I felt the blood drain from my face into my feet while my body went cold. The words echoed in my head. My legs were gone. Somehow, I asked Nicola to repeat what she just said. "I was told that Patrick was shot, and I am with his family on the way to the city morgue to identify the body." I took a deep breath, then told her to hang in there and call me as soon as she knew for sure that he was dead. As soon as I got off the phone, I made plans to go straight to Patrick's neighbourhood. I needed to be there, on the streets, with our folks. While I was getting ready to go, thousands of questions filled my mind. Instantly, I went into denial, thinking that this was one bad dream. A nightmare that would go away once I woke up. But soon common sense took over. *How could this be? How could such a great guy like "Blue Boy" be shot?* He was the last person on earth that I thought would get killed by a gang. He wasn't the type of person who had anything to do with them.

Patrick's only connection to the gang lifestyle was that he lived in a neighbourhood that had a reputation for gang activity.

Patrick's community is full of wonderful, caring and loving people but there are a few involved in criminal behaviour. This is the sad fact of life in "at-risk" neighbourhoods. Innocent people are more susceptible to getting hurt by the repercussions from the illegal activity that takes place within the community. Now it seemed that Patrick might be one of the innocent victims.

I am the executive director of UrbanPromise Toronto,[1] an inner-city ministry that serves children, youth and their mothers in "high-risk" communities in our city. As an urban worker, I understand the complicated pressures many inner-city dwellers face on a day-to-day basis. Most of the people I know living in the city are outstanding citizens. Yet crime, violence and drug abuse has a grasp on these urban neighbourhoods, deeply impacting the wonderful people who live there. The tragic irony is that most crime that takes place in these communities comes from people who enter the neighbourhood from outside. Criminal activity, such as drug dealing, persists in many inner-city communities simply because richer folk feed into the drug industry as they drive in from the outer suburbs to the 'hood to buy drugs. This outside influence and demand keeps the drug trade profitable. The insatiable desire to seek a high through drug use creates employment opportunities specifically appealing to young men who have few financial alternatives or options to make money in socially acceptable ways. If the demand were to dry up, so would the drug dealing. Unfortunately, the demand will always be present.

This feeds the temptation for desperate young men to deal drugs and join gangs for control of the drug trade. When this happens, violence occurs and often innocent people are caught in the middle.

When you work the streets, you come to understand that the local dealer is really a little pawn with a short lifespan. The real criminals in all of this mess are the buyers, who keep the supply and demand flowing so there is a market, and the kingpin, who provides the drugs to be sold. This supplier is the one who goes unscathed and makes the money while the foot soldiers on the streets, who do his dealings, end up in jail or in the grave. The buyers and the supplier, the two key criminal elements who keep the drug industry going strong, often do not live in the actual community that is affected by their illicit dealings.

A number of young men living in low-income neighbourhoods feel they have little hope for the future and fall prey to the "easy life" of drug dealing. They are the perfect suckers, primed by our society of rejection to be easy targets for drug suppliers. These young people are used by the supplier to make money for *him* by becoming his resident drug dispensers on the streets. They are bigger victims than the buyers who are addicted to what they sell. The end result of all of this is that many innocent people who reside in these communities are forced to struggle with stereotypical negative media coverage that harms their reputations and, in far too many cases, results in death.

It is a sad fact that many of the youth with whom we work with are easily drawn into the gang lifestyle. In many poorer communities, the thug life can be very appealing. To many of our desperate young people, it seems to be the only option they have. I remember reading an interview with the famous "gangsta rapper" 50 Cent, whose real name is Curtis Jackson. He is famous for his gritty raps about money, sex and violence. On his web site, you can see pictures of him with photographs of various types of guns. He even starred in a Hollywood movie based loosely on his life. The title of the movie aptly describes the mantra of many urban gangstas: *Get Rich or Die Tryin'*. The problem is that no one seems to notice that most die trying.

50 Cent knows what he is rapping about, as he once was a drug dealer himself. The various bullet hole scars left on his body tell a tale of gang life. He has become a role model for many low-income youth as a man who has "kept it real" with his true street credentials. In this interview, 50 Cent explains why urban young people get involved in criminal activity. We can learn much from 50 Cent regarding the pressures facing our low-income youth who live in "at-risk" communities that are void of many positive alternatives. This is what he says in the interview:

> "Where I'm from, when you tell people you're hungry, instead of giving you fish they give you a pole. Cause they know if I'm asking for a pair of sneakers right now, because it's cool to have that pair of sneakers, two weeks from now I'm going to want another pair. So, instead of giving me $100 they gave me 3 $1/2$ grams of cocaine and permission to sell it in the area. When you tell a kid that's 12 years old, that's having a hard time in school, 'If you do good in school for 8 more years you can have the things that you're after'—and he sees someone in his neighbourhood who got it in a few months hustling—it doesn't seem like one of the options, it seems like the only option." (Rapper 50 Cent)[2]

We live in a culture that overwhelmingly pressures young people to believe that they are nothing unless they wear a certain brand or drive a specific car. True success is based not on character but on how many materialistic baubles one has in his or her possession. The pressures of our "bling, bling," money-oriented society creates temptations that are much stronger for a youth who faces poverty, racism, police profiling and cultural stereotyping. Can you really blame a kid who lives below the poverty line and has no options that many upper class youth have for caving into the gang-life mentality? For them, it seems that everyone is opposed to them, and with the odds stacked against them, why not lash out and do it alone? When those who live in low-income communities seemingly have friends who now have all the trappings of materialistic success the easy way through dealing drugs, why not give into the temptation and join them? After all, the legitimate way to make it in life leads through college or university, but with the extremely high tuition costs and with many family members who have never had the chance to attend a place of higher learning, how can a poor kid ever afford or be motivated to try post-secondary education?

With limited hope, many at-risk youth feel that they might as well drop out of school and make money some other way. They are not dumb, and they know that there are two ways to success—the hard route through school and jobs (which is full of a multitude of obstacles), or the easy way through criminal activity. They understand that in their society it is not *what* you know that counts, but *whom* that matters, and unfortunately for them they do not know the right people.

From their negative life experiences, urban youth know very well that in order to succeed in school and in the marketplace one must have "social capital." They have seen many (less qualified) people gain job opportunities and college acceptance interviews not because of their character but because they knew people in high places. Because of this, the other route, a life of crime, often seems like the only viable option for them. It is for this reason that many gang members actually believe what they do is a legitimate lifestyle that is reserved for those who lack the "social capital" that many upper-class individuals have. Just those terms "upper class" and "lower class" say it all. Who ever came up with this discriminatory terminology and why has it been accepted in our day-to-day conversation? Who gives anyone the right to say that the poor are "lower class" and the rich are "upper class"? Yet the sad thing is these terms are totally acceptable in a society that attempts to keep people locked into neat categories that enslave them to a life of lower-class living.

At-risk youth look at all of this and say to themselves: "This is wrong and I refuse to play by their rules. I am not lower-class, and I will make it in life my way and by my rules!" They are angry at this great injustice and rightfully so, for it is wrong to be labelled by such terms. Unfortunately, without hope and social capital, they feel that there is no other option for them to escape the labels they have been stuck with from birth. All they think they have going for them is the "street life" that is available to them staring them right in the eye as a luring temptation.

It is with this knowledge and empathy towards our youth that I often pray that God would keep them safe from gangs, as many face seemingly insurmountable odds simply because they live in the 'hood. Each time I hear of another gang-related shooting in the city, my antennae go up. This is because in the back of my mind I have a list of names and faces that I know are into trouble and could easily get themselves seriously hurt or killed.

I remember reading the newspaper one day and seeing the face of one of the youths I had personally mentored when I was a youth worker 12 years earlier. He was a real nice kid, quiet and introspective, but very eager to please. Unfortunately, he had got caught up in drugs and slowly disappeared from my life. The article was describing how he was involved in a gruesome murder. Apparently, he killed a businessman who had paid him to provide sexual favours. What this sad story did not mention was how this young man lived a tormented life as a child after being given up for adoption as a baby. Whatever inner turmoil he faced was soothed by his use of illegal drugs, and in time he became so addicted to crack that he was selling himself as a male prostitute in order to get money to support his drug habit. The article went on to state that he had stabbed his "john" over forty times with a knife and was arrested shortly after the police found him driving aimlessly around the city in the victim's car. With my background knowledge of this young man's life, I understood the anger that was so violently displayed in each swing of the knife that he placed into his victim's chest. Over 40 wounds! For every violent act there is usually a sad story left unsaid.

Yes, I had my list of names and faces of teens who desired to live the over-hyped "thug" life, but "Blue Boy" was not on that list. Patrick was shot simply because he was in the wrong place at the wrong time. But how could he be any place else—he lived there! He was one of the many innocent and good citizens.

Patrick was on staff with us and one of our finest StreetLeaders, a perfect poster child for our StreetLeader program. This program allows us to hire young people from the community to work with us as after-school tutors and summer camp counsellors and is a powerful tool providing leadership, self-esteem and job skill development for inner-city youth. It also provides a positive outlet for their energies where they can give back to their communities and, at the same time, get paid for doing what is right. Our StreetLeaders are incredible role models who have become heroes to the children in their neighbourhoods. Now the gangs plaguing these communities have some competition—our UrbanPromise StreetLeader program.

Patrick was a 19-year-old tutor and summer camp counsellor who had worked with us for four years. This was no criminal. He was committed to his work and had a genuine love for the kids with whom he worked. Often, when he wasn't scheduled to work with us, he would still come anyway, volunteering his time just so he could be with his kids that he loved so much. Every time I saw him, he had a pile of kids draped all over him. Kids hanging off his back, arms and legs, all laughing together in a giant walking mass of humanity as he slowly dragged them around the community centre where our program took place. When life was hard on the kids, they felt safe running into his strong and loving arms.

I knew there was no way that Patrick was involved in any criminal activity. He was simply a victim of his circumstances, of mistaken identity, another of the many risks that our youth must deal with while living in communities where drugs, gangs and violence are far too present.

My wife Judith heard my distressed voice on the phone and knew what had happened. She had our children in her arms, and they were already praying. I joined them for quick prayer and gave them a hug, grateful to God for the blessing of life He had given to my family. Then I grabbed my car keys, ran out the door, screeched out of my driveway and drove the 15-minute drive to Patrick's community without a clue of what I was about to encounter or how I was going to be of any help.

My brain kept trying to wake up from this horrible nightmare. But the reality of it all came crashing down. Denial, disbelief, then adrenaline, racing to get to Patrick's neighbourhood, to be with his kids, his friends and family, searching for something to do or say that would make things okay. But they weren't okay, and they wouldn't be for a long, long time. I cried and yelled at God the whole way there.

The whole thing was wrong and unfair. There was nothing I could do to save "Blue Boy's" life. All I knew was that I had to be there, in his community, walking his streets, being with his people—all the while waiting for the phone call to tell me if Patrick was indeed dead.

---

1 UrbanPromise also operates in Camden, New Jersey, Wilmington, Delaware and Vancouver, British Columbia, Canada. To receive more information on UrbanPromise Toronto, please go to www.urbanpromise.com.

2 Rapper 50 Cent, taken from a *Toronto Star* interview. "A Great Deal for 50 Cent" by Ashante Infantry, July 12, 2003.

---◆---

"For this people's heart has become calloused; they hardly hear with their ears, and they have closed their eyes. Otherwise they might see with their eyes, hear with their ears, understand with their hearts and turn, and I would heal them."

– Matthew 13:15 (NIV)

HE WHO HAS EYES TO SEE

◆

CHAPTER TWO

It is a short distance from my house to the Warden Woods community where Patrick lived. However, on that day the drive seemed like an eternity. Every traffic light, every stop sign and any slow-moving car that got in my way became a lightning rod for my wrath. I was emotionally on edge. I could not get the words out of my head: "'Blue Boy' has been shot." It made no sense. He was not a gangbanger. He was not a criminal. He had no links whatsoever to any criminal activity. *Why him?* He was soft-spoken, shy and always smiling. He was, in the words of so many people in his community, the one who was going to make it. He had enrolled in college, gave back to his community by working with children, and was an all-around positive light and role model to the children he served at UrbanPromise. And now this? *Was this a cruel joke? Was I experiencing a horrible nightmare that would go away once I awoke?* No, this was reality. I cursed, wept and prayed the whole way to Warden Woods.

I pulled up to the community centre and parked my car. All of a sudden, a wave of fear and apprehension came over me. *Was it really Patrick? Was it one of our kids?* I remained for a minute or two in the safety of my car, anxious about what I would encounter on the streets in Patrick's Warden Woods neighbourhood. All sorts of apprehensive questions danced in my head. *How would I handle my staff, who would be deeply devastated by the news that their friend may be a murder victim? What would I say to the weeping children who idolized Patrick? How could I console his family? In what ways would I be able to offer comfort to the people of his community?*

29

I was scared. I had no idea what to do. I sent up a quick prayer to God asking for His power, and then I resolved to get out of the car. Opening the door of my black Honda Civic, I weakly gulped some air and swallowed hard. I then slowly made my way up the path into the community centre. When I walked into the building, I was greeted by a spattering of dazed, zombie-like creatures staring into space. The receptionist sitting behind the large desk in the main hallway looked relieved when she saw me walking through the front doors. It was obvious from her fearful and strained expression that she was doing her best to deal with the hurting people all around her. It was even more evident that she felt totally inept in her attempts to provide comfort.

Her eyes lit up when I entered the room, and I could just hear her thoughts through her expressive, worried eyes: "Finally, the professional is here to take over and make everyone feel better." To her, I was the person who could deal with this crisis. I was supposed to wave my magic wand and, through my powers, words and presence, make sense of and bring healing to the pain everyone was feeling in this close-knit community. Little did she know that the apparently strong and composed figure she saw standing in front of her was partly an optical illusion. On the outside, I must have looked calm, cool and collected. But on the inside, I was far from it.

To those I encountered that night, I was a walking mirage, a deceptive oasis brought about by their misplaced hope for something to quench their desperate craving for relief. In truth, I was just another scared presence, standing lost and forlorn, within the maze of lifeless faces that were all around me. The secretary excitedly waved me into a room, saying that my staff members were in there alone and they were waiting for me. I went in and we all hugged, wept and prayed. We still hadn't heard any news, still didn't know if our precious friend was alive or dead. There we were, broken people, weakened by the stress of the unknown. Yet, something supernatural was among us.

There was a strength, the strength of being together, knowing that we were *not* alone, knowing that together we could get through this. Though no one said it at the time, we knew that we were all experiencing the same thing. We were hurting, but underneath our pain was a current of God's presence. He was there. And He was suffering with us.

Nicola called again. It was confirmed that Patrick Dalton Pitters was one of three murder victims killed on the city streets that evening of March 4, 2004. Until then, we were hoping that whoever had been shot had been misidentified and that it wasn't Patrick. But this was real. Upon hearing the news, some of my staff cried quietly, others stared into space, a few wept out loud, one collapsed on the floor in grief. All of us prayed.

Apparently, Patrick died while visiting an apartment that was not in his community. He was invited by a friend to play video games at the apartment of a drug dealer. Patrick did not know the owner was a dealer.

During the evening, while he was playing video games, some men broke into the apartment with guns, looking for the dealer. A fight ensued, but Patrick didn't get involved. He sat glued to the couch, clutching his game controller, confused and not knowing what was happening in front of him. During the fight, a shotgun fired twice, hitting Patrick in the chest twice as he sat, stunned, on the couch. The gunmen ran and Patrick's friends quickly took him to the nearest hospital.

He was dead on arrival.

We spent the night in the community, as it offered us a strange solace. People came in and out of the community centre seeking comfort they received through fellow sufferers. UrbanPromise staff went throughout the neighbourhood on little walks and spontaneous prayer meetings erupted on the streets in the community.

People were tuned into the spiritual world like never before and it was common to witness complete strangers hugging each other while huddling together in prayer. From the toughest men to the most vulnerable children, everyone in the community was humbled, broken and open to God. Our God, familiar with suffering, had now come close to that community in Warden Woods. He was definitely present in every nook and cranny. His Spirit was hovering over the streets and moving among the people there. Though we were all experiencing the devastating results of sin, God's grace was even more present, slowly oozing out His healing comfort. Where sin abounds, grace abounds more (Romans 5:20).

It is only human to do all we can to avoid suffering. Yet ironically God seems to be most present in our tears. In 2 Corinthians 1:3-5, Paul states:

> "Praise be to the God and Father of our Lord Jesus Christ, the Father of compassion and the **God of all comfort, who comforts us in all our troubles,** so that we can comfort those in any trouble with the comfort we ourselves have received from God. For **just as the sufferings of Christ flow over into our lives, so also through Christ our comfort overflows.**" (NIV, emphasis added)

God's comforting goes hand in hand with suffering. You can't have one without the other. Suffering, though unpleasant at the time, is a reality of life. It is guaranteed—we will all go through it. Suffering is inevitable in a sinful world. We should not be surprised when we go through afflictions. In fact, we should expect it.

However, there is good news. Linked to suffering is comfort. Comfort of others when we suffer together, and more importantly, that of God's presence in the midst of our suffering. Jesus is found in the midst of our pain. In His immense grace, He enters our suffering and provides comfort for those who open their hearts to Him. Jesus does not leave us alone, but actually joins us in our tears. The tears we weep become His. The pain we feel becomes His pain. He actually embodies each emotion we feel and carries our hurt even more deeply than we ever feel it. He does this for every person, everywhere, at anytime, throughout the world. Jesus weeps with the mother who loses her child to disease in the Third World. He cries with every father who loses his son to AIDS. He feels the pain in the heart of every rape victim or every child who loses a parent to the ravages of war. He lovingly understands the painful and convoluted thought process of every pregnant teenaged girl who chooses to abort her child while, at the same time, experiencing the pain of every unborn child and the wasted future that could have been.

This is the God of all comfort, the God of all love, the God of all grace. For on the cross, Jesus took up our infirmities and carried our sorrows. He is now linked forever to the suffering of those He gave Himself for. He was pierced for our transgressions, He was crushed for our iniquities and by His wounds we are healed (Isaiah 53:4,5). He also is the great High Priest who sympathizes with our weaknesses and who is able to deal gently with those who are ignorant and have gone astray (Hebrews 4:15,16; 5:1,2). This Jesus, the eternal now, sees all suffering and, because of who He is, cannot turn a blind eye to what He sees. The same love that drove Jesus to the cross remains today and He cannot walk away from our suffering, but is bound by His love for us to experience the pain we suffer in even greater depths.

Jesus is like a loving mother, whose heart aches over her sick child and who wishes she could change places with her daughter to provide relief. Jesus feels our pain to a greater extent than we could ever experience it. It is because of the reality of this emotional and grieving God that I feel comfortable enough to approach Him for help. The marvelous thing is that I usually don't have to go too far to receive comfort from Him as He is already present in my grief. God runs to us before our first tear falls. In fact, *His* tears for us have already fallen before *ours* well up in our eyes. This is why I can trust God—He has tears in His eyes and nail scars in His hands and feet. This is the God who is approachable to those who sin, as well as those who suffer its repercussions.

Grief and love are inseparable. If we love, we will hurt. In fact, the more we love, the more we hurt. Loving people means setting yourself up for major pain. Love causes you to become attached to the one you love. This attachment is real and results in a sharing of emotions (happy and sad) and even physical pain. (There are many cases where a child suffers pain and the parents experience that same pain.) People in love want what is best for each other and receive joy when good things happen. However, the opposite is also true. When they suffer, you suffer. This sharing of emotions and experience of collective pain is a strong proof that you love. To really impact someone's life, love is required. This is why God has such a powerful impact on our lives.

God loves us and because of this He doesn't only laugh and cry with us, but most importantly, His love transforms us. For love to work at its highest potency, it must be connected to those who suffer. If we love, we are willing to enter another's afflictions and suffer with them. We must experience their pain, their injustice, their nightmares. When this happens, we demonstrate our love to them, for love limited to spoken words is cheap and is not love at all. Love, for it to have an impact, must be manifested through our shared experience.

"Greater love has no one than this, that he lay down his life for his friends." (John 15:13, NIV)

Love is proven when it is connected to sacrificial suffering.

If I have any integrity with those we serve at UrbanPromise, it is only because I have gone through some of the suffering with which our people must deal. I have witnessed first-hand the issues of racism, injustice, abuse and the various indignities that poverty produces in their lives. It is during these times I have come to appreciate the symbolism in the Roman Catholic crucifix. This is because I can better relate to the crucifix of the suffering Jesus than to the cross that has been emptied by my Protestant brethren. I find it very comforting to know that we have a God who is familiar with injustice, poverty and suffering. He is the Jesus who truly suffered on the cross. Suffered for our sins. And suffers now with us in our brokenness.

He doesn't hide from suffering but embraces it and has experienced every type of suffering known to man. I am so glad that in times of trials I can come to this Jesus, my God, who

"...was despised and rejected by men, a man of sorrows, and **familiar with suffering.**" (Isaiah 53:3, NIV, emphasis added)

Did you get that last part? *He is familiar with suffering.* He is approachable because He is with us in our pain. He has been there. He still is there. This is the type of God to which the poor can relate—the One who hangs on a cross, the One who suffers with us, the One who has and still does face injustice and indignity. The One who was born in poverty. Christ is love because He chose to go through more suffering than we could ever experience. He has confirmed the deep integrity of His love by choosing to suffer to the greatest extent for us. He still does. This suffering Jesus is the Saviour that we fellow sufferers can easily approach. He has proven His love by undeservedly dying on the cross for us (Romans 5:8).

While suffering Patrick's loss, we felt a deep chasm of emptiness in our hearts. Together, we were all grieving the loss of a friend and loved one. What made our suffering even worse was the fact that Patrick had been murdered, and some in the media were assuming his guilt as a gangbanger. They couldn't have been more wrong. Murder is such a heinous act of evil, and when it happens to a young man just entering his prime, an innocent victim, it is painfully hard to deal with. Someone stole his life in the midst of what seemed to be a path that would lead to life-changing moments for everyone he touched.

Of all the types of grief to bear, the loss of a loved one to murder has to be the toughest. We all needed the gentle touch of the God of all comfort and He was not letting us down! We felt His presence in each hug offered and received, with each tearful glance and in the prayers we had together. In the midst of this injustice, Jesus was right there, suffering with us. Somehow, there was peace in the midst of all this craziness because we knew that though God was not responsible for the actions of the murderers, He was not absent from our dilemma. The horrible, sinful actions performed by the few cannot stop God from making beautiful things happen. God's kingdom is still being fully established. He was present in it all.

Later that night, I went home and began preparing for crisis counselling for our staff and the children whom Patrick served. They needed it and so did I. It was a hard night. My own children were traumatized and had nightmares (this continued for months afterwards) that a bad man would break into our house and murder us in our sleep. After a restless night, I arrived, bright and early, back at the community centre and was greeted at the door by the media. The place was crawling with cameras, reporters and huge television network vans with satellite dishes on their roofs. As I brushed them aside and made my way into the centre, I heard a teenager utter the following words, while pointing angrily at the media throng:

"Why are they always here when something bad happens? Why are they not here when all the good stuff occurs like when one of us graduates from school? They should have been here a long time ago, doing a story on Patrick, a good story, instead of this one."

I remember talking to the media later in the day and asked them why they never seemed to report on the many good news stories that took place on a regular basis in our communities. I shouldn't have been surprised by the response. I was told that there is far more bad news taking place than good in our city, and therefore the media report only what they see. "How sad!" I replied. "You are blind because you do not see that there are far more good news stories out here than bad. You are so blind to goodness that all you can see is evil."

How do you see goodness? Love. Love provides true 20/20 vision because it tends to see things differently. Love sees the truth. Love sees the good news stories in spite of the bad.

I remember hearing Dr. Tony Campolo, founder of UrbanPromise, telling a story of his teaching days at the University of Pennsylvania where he was a professor of sociology. During one of his lectures, Tony made reference to Jesus' ministry to prostitutes. It was then that he was challenged by one of his students, who curtly disrupted the lecture by proclaiming that Jesus never saw a prostitute in His entire life. Tony, rather agitated by this young man's audacity to not only interrupt his teaching but also challenge his intellect, took on the young man in front of the class and began to share Scripture that showed Jesus' ministry of compassion to prostitutes. Tony was experiencing enormous satisfaction as he ripped into this pretentious student, defending the faith while impressing his students with his great knowledge.

When he was finished with the student, he knew he had won the argument and saved the day for the cause of Christ. His reputation was intact and his respect level with the students had risen with each word that left his scholarly tongue. Tony smirked smugly, knowing that he had proved that Jesus saw not just one, but many prostitutes in His day. However, the tables were quickly turned and Tony was left speechless when the student replied, "Dr. Campolo, you see a prostitute in those Bible passages you just read. The people who were with Jesus in the Scriptures you shared also saw Jesus hanging out with prostitutes. To you and them, all you see are whores. But do you really think Jesus saw them that way? Do you think Jesus saw them as whores or two-bit prostitutes? When Jesus looked into the eyes of a prostitute, do you really think He saw a prostitute or did He see a beautiful child of God?"

Ouch! This student was not only bold, he was right and Tony knew it. It was true. Jesus never saw prostitutes, He only saw children of God. Jesus, walking on the streets of our cities today, does not see bums, winos, hookers, drug addicts or gangbangers. He sees His created children, His brothers and sisters, His lost sheep. He sees God's beauty marks all over each hurting, marginalized or so-called successful person His eyes come across. Love sees things differently.

The Jewish mystics teach us well about this concept of sight that is only made available through love. There is a story[1] they tell to describe the glory of God. These mystics viewed God's *shekina* (Hebrew for glory) as the wife of God. They taught that at creation, God and his *shekina* were united in close harmony. All of creation beamed with the *shekina* glory of God. However, after the Fall of mankind, when sin entered the world, His *shekina* was disturbed. God was separated from it and it was imprisoned inside the fallen creation. The question then is: *How does God reunite with his shekina?* The answer of the mystics is that *shekina* is freed through the deeds of the righteous. Righteous people are God's instruments that can release and free the *shekina* imprisoned in creation by their virtuous acts.

In other words, God's glory, His *shekina*, is all around us, entrapped in every created and living thing. Our lives then become an exciting adventure of freeing up God's glory through our acts of kindness. In this way, love sees things differently. This is why I cannot help but see *shekina* all around me as I walk the streets of the communities in which we work, neighbourhoods that others have labelled dark and dangerous. I see God's wonderful glory present, just waiting to burst out all around me. God's *shekina* is on the streets of your city too, if you choose to look at it with the eyes of Jesus—with eyes of love. It is present in the form of a homeless youth who begs for spare change. It is active in the hands of the crack addict who places a quarter in his cup. It manifests itself in the businessman's smile as he places a $20 bill in the same beggar's cup. It is heard in the voice of the beggar who responds by saying, "Thank you for your kindness."

The wisdom of Proverbs teaches us some very interesting truths about the importance of seeing. In Proverbs 11:27, we read: "He who seeks good finds goodwill, but evil comes to him who searches for it" (NIV).

The lesson here is simple and yet profound. Goodness and evil are empowered according to how much they are sought out and desired. If you seek out goodness, you will find it and in return will receive it in ongoing abundance in your life. The opposite is also true. If all you seek is evil, then evil is what you will find—it will increase. The more evil we speak about, the more evil we tend to see we will eventually emulate. In the neighbourhoods where we are active, the lie of evil is so strong that many young people actually tend to believe that evil is good and good is evil. Goodness has become archaic and unpractical, and the code of the streets is that if you are not evil, then someone will take advantage of you. The only way to survive is to be more evil than the next person. Thus the old saying "Only the good die young" becomes a reality. This problem multiplies quickly in our society when you consider the influence of the media via print, television and radio that seeks evil to broadcast. If it is true that evil sells papers, then we are in big trouble. Evil has great PR, and it results in people being afraid and feeling hopeless. When this happens, life becomes a game of self-survival by all means necessary and selfishness is the epitome of evil.

The solution to this mess is to have proper eyesight. The Church must be involved in our city, seeing God's *shekina* that just waits to be loosed from the shackles of evil. The Church must have Jesus' eyes to see it. It must also understand it is uniquely gifted for this endeavour. The writer of Proverbs continues to give us more insight on this topic of goodness and evil:

> "With his mouth the godless destroys his neighbour but through knowledge the righteous escape. Through the blessing of the upright a city is exalted, but by the mouth of the wicked it is destroyed. A man who lacks judgement derides his neighbour, but a man of understanding holds his tongue." (Proverbs 11:9,11,12, NIV)

These verses of wisdom tell us that the social, moral and spiritual health of our cities and neighbourhoods is based on what the upright, in comparison to the godless, are doing. More directly, the welfare of our cities rests on how the upright see the city. God is present all around us and with true godly understanding one can see His presence in the 'hood. God's *shekina* is there.

It always breaks my heart when I hear of another shooting in my city. It especially hurts when I hear Christians deride the neighbourhood where the shooting took place by saying things like "What do you expect from that place? I would never go there. It is a ghetto, an awful community." Whenever I hear these types of comments from Christians, I cannot help but think of the verse from Proverbs we just read.

Think of what people say about the tough neighbourhoods in *your* city. Is it any wonder they remain hotspots of evil? Parts of our cities are dangerous simply because they lack our blessing because Christians have abandoned them. And this is to our shame. We hear of the evil that occurs there and we either flee those communities directly (I know of one community in my city that has had over 20 churches shut down and leave within 20 years—the true plight of the inner-city Church), or else we target them as hit-and-run ministry projects. Hit them with a prayer walk or one-day event and then run away as far as possible. Instead, what we need to do is stay in the community, work with the community, and have long-term, practical, relationally-based ministry in the community. When this happens, you see the many good and God things present there, and you cannot help but bless the city.

---

[1] M. Frost and A. Hirsch, *The Shaping of Things to Come—Innovation and Mission for the 21st-Century Church*, Hendrickson Publishers, Peabody, Massachusetts, 2003, p.128.

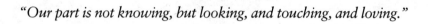

"Our part is not knowing, but looking, and touching, and loving."

– Unknown

HOW GOD SHOWS UP

◆

CHAPTER THREE

Patrick lived in a government housing community that would be labelled *the projects* or *the 'hood*. Only a few years ago this neighbourhood was branded a violent community in which drug-related turf wars were common. It was so bad that the community centre located in the neighbourhood used to gauge the success of its programs in accordance with the number of murders that occurred in the community. If there were just a few during the year, it reckoned that it was a successful year. However, if that wasn't the case, the centre would then have to re-evaluate the effectiveness of its programs. In the previous five years, there hadn't been one murder, and the reasons for this successful statistic could be accredited to two sources.

First, there was Kwendie, a tough-as-nails African-Canadian youth worker who had put in many years, tears and love into the lives of the youth of Warden Woods. She was both a mother and father figure for the teens in the community and she never had a problem physically confronting the youth when they were out of line. Though small, she is large in heart, and because of this she could confront the toughest young men in the community with confidence, knowing that they would back down under her brooding glare. She was the embodiment of tough love, a proven advocate for her boys in the 'hood. She had gained the right to speak into the lives of the young men in her community simply because she had proven herself a veteran youth worker, willing to tough it out even in the worst of circumstances. When the youth were little children she was always there watching out for them. Now that they had grown into young adults she was still present and available—a living and breathing anchor of stability and hope in the community. Her love for the youth was seen in that she knew every one of them by name. She was the real deal, a genuine, caring and tough guide. In return, the youth listened to her as she was revered by every one of them. She had earned their respect and it was well deserved.

The second factor was the emergence of UrbanPromise. Many people in the community have told me that they have noticed a huge difference in the ethos of the neighbourhood ever since UrbanPromise has been involved. In fact, there is a direct correlation between the end of murders and the start of our program. Since we have been in Warden Woods, no one has been killed there! (This includes Patrick. Though he was from this community, he was gunned down outside of the neighbourhood in another housing project a few miles away.)

Over the years, I have come to understand that positive community change is not the result of any sophisticated children's or youth after-school or summer camp programs we operate. It is also not because we run a fancy mothers' program. In fact, our programs are not that fancy at all. We operate a bare-bones program light on the programmatic side, but heavy on the relational and love side. What we lack in ornate bells and whistles and fancy, expensive programming is well made up with loving care from our staff. We, like Kwendie, earn respect through our commitment, dedication and genuine love for our people. Simply stated, our programs are just vehicles that allow loving relationships to take place. To us, they are not the be all and end all, but simply a means to the end, which is to create a loving and gracious environment where God's power flows. Our task is not to run programs, but to craft an ethos of love and grace. Our goal is to create holy places where the love of God can be experienced. These holy places are safe environments where children, youth and mothers can be real and share their heart struggles with each other without fear of judgement or slander.

It is evident to all those who live in Warden Woods that the community has changed for the better simply because God is present through love. Influences like Kwendie and UrbanPromise have brought so much love into the community. By being instruments of love, God is more present than ever before.

"God is love." (1 John 4:16, NIV)

It cannot get any simpler. It is not a secret—God shows up when love is present. We are making a difference in these communities simply because God is manifesting Himself in the love that is present through the relationships that take place in our programs. By allowing love to flow from our staff to those we serve, we also are seeing love reciprocated among the children, youth and their mothers. Our community is a tremendous group of people who have the opportunity to break out of the fear so often present in marginalized communities. Love is the antidote to fear.

Though we may have brought love into the community, we have also discovered that there are many wonderful people living there who also have a lot of love to share. Together, through love, we are all experiencing God. The results are astounding as we are seeing entire families transformed. Hope is restored, not only *to* those we serve, but also *from* those we serve. God is definitely in the community, and it is His *shalom* (peace) that is making a difference. This is the secret of ministry. Not more elaborate programs. Not more costly facilities. Not more rules of conduct or more PhDs. Just lots of love.

It is refreshing to know that those of us who cannot afford to build massive buildings or attend prestigious places of higher learning can still have the most powerful transformative tool at our disposal—God's love. Our mission as Christians is quite simple and that is to unleash God through love. John 3:16 is a loud declaration of God's mission plan of love when He sent His Son to us:

"For God so loved the world that He gave *(or unleashed love)* His Son."

This ministry strategy of love was lived out in the person of Jesus. Everywhere He went, He loved. Contrarily, the religious leaders of His day believed that the way to do ministry was to manipulate and rule with power and fear over the people with all types of religious rules, laws and programs. Jesus shattered their strategies by His loving actions as He boldly declared, "the kingdom of God is near" (Luke 10:9, NIV). How? The answer is simple—look at Jesus. The kingdom manifests itself on two fronts: loving words and loving actions. Jesus preached love through what He said and also by what He did. When you study His life, you discover that His love wasn't just talk. It was also communicated by His lifestyle.

You can read His loving words as recorded in the Gospels. Better yet, you can see His loving actions concretely through His healings and acceptance of those who were deemed unclean and unacceptable by the religious ruling party of His day. There are many lessons here for how we, as Jesus' followers, are to speak and live.

First John 4:16 states: "God is love." John doesn't say that God just speaks love. John states that God is *love*. In other words, every thought God has, every act in which He participates, every thing He sees automatically occurs through the lens of love. Love is who He is. It is not limited only to what He does or says.

The disciples and Paul continued this ministry strategy of love. We read in the Book of Acts how the early Church members loved each other through practical examples of sharing meals together and caring for the poor and the widows. What were the results of this love in action? The Church grew rapidly and in quick succession. Many people were impacted, not only because of the apostles' preaching, but also because their preaching was accompanied by actions of love. Just like Jesus—loving words and loving actions.

In 1 Corinthians 13, Paul stresses the pre-eminence of love in all we do. It is important for us to understand the context in which he wrote these words. This passage of Scripture is part of a letter Paul wrote to the church in Corinth that he had founded on his second missionary journey. Shortly after he left them, they slowly fell apart in schisms fueled by pride, immorality and lawsuits. In other words, this was a church that clearly lacked love. In response to the factions and anger within this church, Paul pens the inspired and famous love chapter. He hits the nail on the head when he writes:

"Love is patient, love is kind. It does not envy, it does not boast, it is not proud. It is not rude, it is not self-seeking, it is not easily angered, it keeps no record of wrongs. Love does not delight in evil but rejoices with the truth. It always protects, always trusts, always hopes, always perseveres.... And now these three remain: faith, hope and love. But the greatest of these is love." (1 Corinthians 13:4-7,13, NIV)

This isn't just flowery, poetic literature to be read at weddings. This is dynamite we are dealing with here. Explosive material that can impact people's lives, communities, cities and countries! These simple verses on love, which so many of us have heard many times before, are powerful truths that we need to live out in our lives, communities, work places, schools, ministries and churches. They must be a priority. Do you see how practical love is? According to Paul, love is not a feeling but action. Love without action is nothing. But love with action is the greatest of all things.

I believe there is a love famine happening in our society. Too many of our schools, businesses, gathering places, churches and ministries lack this priority of love. The goal for too many of our organizations and businesses has been based on business strategies that lack the need for an ethos and culture where love flourishes. Our CEOs may have great organizational charts, goals and profit strategies, but what they lack is the substance of love. This is seen so often when companies reward their CEOs with obscene bonuses in the millions of dollars for running huge profits and making their stockholders happy at the cost of laying off thousands of workers. Something is wrong when this is seen as success, where the few get rich while many lose their jobs. In their eyes it is clear that the bottom-line definition of success is not how people are treated, but how much stocks go up. Where is the love? I sincerely wonder what would happen to a company that emphasized love as "the greatest of these" over and above greed. I think the company would not only succeed financially but soulfully as well.

"If I speak in the tongues of men and of angels, but have not love, I am only a resounding gong or a clanging cymbal." (1 Corinthians 13:1 NIV)

If we lack love, we are like a resounding gong. Have you ever heard a gong clanging? Now imagine this happening non-stop. It would be like having to sit in a classroom while someone scraped nails down the blackboard for hours on end. It would drive you insane and cause you to cover your ears, wrinkle your nose and run away, as fast as possible, from this awful resounding racket. Yet this is exactly how Paul describes what unloving people and unloving companies or organizations are like in the eyes and ears of God. If we do not care for people it is a horrible clanging gong in the ears of God.

Unfortunately, sound also reverberates in places that should be havens of love, and the repercussions are devastating. This dearth of love is not only a problem in the dog-eat-dog business world, but it far too often is present within our places of worship.

I have the privilege of speaking in many churches and have to admit that, as a speaker, I often repeat the same message in different locales. The reason for this is quite simple. Travelling allows me to speak to different audiences, thus allowing me to repeat certain messages simply because the listeners are different. To the new audience, an old sermon is new.

When you preach as often as I do, most places seem the same and their congregations tend to fade away in your memory. However, I do admit that there are some places I will never forget. Some of these churches are congregations in which you can feel God's presence abiding among His people. They are places that energize you as a speaker, and there just seems to be that extra pizzazz of spiritual dynamism that enters every word you speak. These are wonderful places to visit, and when they ask me to return, I accept their invitation right away. However, there are a few places where I don't like to speak. These are the churches that leave you drained and tired. Speaking at these churches is like a long and tiring wrestling match in which I must tussle with the audience to make the spoken words apply to their hearts.

What is the difference between the two? Why do some energize me while others drain me of every last ounce of energy? The energizing churches are those where love and grace abound through the presence of the Holy Spirit, while the draining churches lack grace and love. The churches that are full of love have no distractions present, and because of this, they can hear God's Word clearly. Churches that lack love have a resounding gong clanging in their midst, distracting them from clearly hearing God's Word.

When I think of this truth, there is one church that stands well above all others. To me, it is the perfect example of the resounding gong syndrome. I'll never forget that day when, with one of my best sermons in tow, I arrived at this church prepared to knock them off their feet. Spiritually speaking, I felt great. I was going through one of those stretches of life where I felt animated daily with God's presence inside me. I was in the midst of a spiritual high and on top of this, I brought a sermon that was one of my top ten hits. I was going to preach one of my time-tested, stellar messages. Everywhere I had previously given this sermon, God seemed to move mightily. I couldn't wait to meet and speak to the people at this church. However, my hopes and dreams for that Sunday were quickly shattered. The message that was so powerful in the past was a dud with this crowd.

I should have known that I was in trouble. The negative signs were clearly evident the very second I entered the church. As I walked through the front doors, I was greeted with a strange feeling of lifelessness. It was obvious to me that something wasn't right.

At first I thought that I was the problem. I did a quick self-examination to find out what condition my soul was in. Perhaps I wasn't doing as well spiritually as I thought. Perhaps there were some unknown spiritual issues I had not dealt with. I quickly walked through the past few days and confessed to the Lord every possible shortcoming that came to mind. I knew that personally I was clean, yet that strange, cold feeling remained. I thought that perhaps what I was feeling was just fatigue or there was some other fairly innocent reason. However, deep in my soul I knew this was not the case. The negative feeling remained. Then it occurred to me. Perhaps the problem wasn't me. Maybe I was unaware of issues present in this church that were so grave, even as an outsider I could feel it. As soon as the worship service began, the feeling of darkness in that place not only remained, but got stronger. It was as if the church was just going through the motions. No one smiled, no one clapped, not one sign of emotion or sign of true worship in that building. The looks on the faces of everyone were cold and robotic. I was staring at lifeless figures sitting together under one roof. A few hymns, a couple of announcements, a solo and then it was my turn to speak. I preached my heart out, but still—no response. The sermon did not seem to be clicking with the audience.

It was as if words left my mouth only to flutter to the ground in a dissolved heap, unable to reach anyone in the front row onwards. There seemed to be no connection between the people in the pews and the words leaving my lips. It was a completely different experience than I had ever encountered. The negative vibe was so strong that I had to struggle through the message.

When I finished my concluding illustration, I was glad that the whole thing was over. All I could think of was getting out of this place as soon as possible. After the final benediction, the pastor came to the pulpit and instructed me to go to the back of the church where I would have the opportunity to greet everyone as they left the service. This was something I did not want to do. The last thing I needed at that time was to shake hands with every cold and lifeless soul who attended this church. Usually, I enjoy meeting new people, but this time all I wanted was to get out of there as quickly as I could. However, there was no escape, no place to run. It was after I had greeted the first few people that I suddenly realized what the problem was and why the feeling in that building was so dark. I was immediately surrounded by angry people who complained incessantly about their pastor. What made it worse was they were using pieces of *my* sermon to vilify and justify their complaints!

Like unethical journalists, they were twisting my words out of context to back up their obvious anti-pastor/church-leadership agenda. I was embarrassed, especially since these complainers were using me as their instrument of destruction right in front of the pastor, who was standing with me as we greeted people!

These people had no love. Love had left that place long ago and when love leaves, God goes with it because He is love. Gossip, manipulation, slandering, backbiting and lack of humility are all annoying gongs that make a church an unpleasant place. Whenever these unloving qualities are present, they should act like a fire alarm, indicating to us that there is a serious crisis at hand.

When love leaves, God's active presence goes with it. When this happens, marriages, families, businesses and even churches are in big trouble. The problem is that too many people have just gotten used to it. It has become an accepted part of life. The strangeness of all these dysfunctional qualities has become normal. Instead of indicating that danger is present, we just ignore the alarm. How contrary this is to the plan of Jesus and to the words of Paul.

Without love, we Christians and our well-financed ministries and well-oiled churches are nothing. What we need to do is invest more energy in love over and above anything else we do. The good news is that love does not cost much money. You can love without blowing the budget.

We need to function with God's power by prioritizing love above all else. To do this, we must come to know how to speak truth with love. When we do, people will "see your good deeds and praise your Father in heaven" (Matthew 5:16, NIV). Now that is a powerful truth.

This is the heartbeat and the blood that flows throughout UrbanPromise—love. We simply love our kids, youth and their mothers, no matter what has happened to them in the past, no matter what they have done or what they are currently doing. We simply love them and because of this, the transcendent God is present, transforming lives as He works through His chosen medium, which is the active presence of love. I am always amazed at how much love we receive in return, not only from the kids and youth with whom we work, but also from their mothers. This love is such a dominant force in our communities that many people who come and visit our programs often tell me that they feel God's presence in our community. This is a common thread felt by newcomers who meet our people for the first time. Many tell me that they are inspired by the children, youth and mothers they meet. It is as if both UrbanPromise staff and those we have come to serve reinforce and energize one another's love for each other.

The communities we serve have taken root in our hearts. My staff eat, breathe and sleep every minute for the people we serve. Though we come from varied backgrounds (Canadian, American, Australian, Asian, Caribbean, Irish, etc.), we all become part of the community in which we are active. This means that we have been absorbed into the Jamaican culture because most neighbourhoods we serve are filled with Jamaican Canadians. Just walk through our communities during the hot summer months and you'll experience the Jamaican "irie." You'll hear the reggae beat playing loudly. You'll see the people gathered together, smiling, high-fiving each other, talking and laughing loudly. There might even be a game of dominoes happening on the front lawn of a townhouse while children skip rope on the street corner. Though our staff might be from a different cultural background, we have all become honourary Jamaicans. Many of us have even come to understand the "patois" way of speaking and enjoy the roti dinners we are served when we are invited, as guests, into the homes of our wonderful families. Often our female staff wear the cornrow hairstyle so fashionable in our communities. This is a real badge of honour—a statement declaring to everyone that a mother in the 'hood spent hours working on their hair. When someone takes the time to do that, you are accepted as part of the community. You are now officially **in**.

Love is visible, and it is also felt. It is seen and experienced through the hospitality present in our communities that defies all stereotypical urban projects, and we receive it with open arms, simply because we have open hearts. We really love those we serve, and this deep affection for our people is seen when you visit one of our staff apartments. As you enter their modest living conditions, you will notice pictures, tons of pictures, of children, youth and mothers, all from these communities. On their bedroom walls, you'll see Bible verses and prayers painted around and about more pictures of these people they have come to love as their own children, brothers, sisters and mothers. Each face in each picture has a name, a story, fears and dreams. They have become part of our family and we have been accepted into their family.

During a day off, it is common to witness one of our staff hanging out with their kids or going to a movie with a mother of a child who attends our program. When my staff talk about the children in **their** program, they never call them kids. No. They are always referred to as "*my* kids." That little word makes all the difference in the world. It speaks of connection, care, love and responsibility. It is clear that the children of UrbanPromise are not just numbers or little projects. They truly **are** our kids. Every day, our staff pray for our kids by name: Shaquan, Shaquille, Aiesha, Sharene, Shevelle, Patrick, and the list goes on. And every day, our kids also pray for us.

"And the greatest of these is love...." (1 Corinthians 13:13)

———————— ◆ ————————

"Our lives are not problems to be solved but journeys to be taken with Jesus as our friend and finest guide."

– Henri Nouwen

THE SECRET POWER OF NOT KNOWING WHAT TO DO

◆

CHAPTER FOUR

One of the many blessings I received while grieving the loss of Patrick was being able to build a stronger friendship with John Elliot, director of the Warden Woods Community Centre, at the time of the tragedy. Before Patrick's murder, John and I were just friends on a casual business basis. After, we became closer friends. Hardships tend to bond sufferers together.

John Elliot was born in Northern Ireland and had worked at the centre for over 15 years. He is a humble man, with a strong Irish accent and an impeccable work ethic, whose love for his staff and the community was obvious. When I think of John, I see a faithful man who made the Warden Woods Community Centre effective in fulfilling its mandate. He always deflected any praise he received and made sure that his staff got proper recognition and encouragement. He empowered them and they in turn respected his guidance.

John arrived at the centre shortly before I did early in the morning after Patrick's murder. When John heard I was in the building, he had his receptionist call me into his office for a quick meeting. I slowly cut through the horde of media, community residents and various hangers-on who crowded around the centre and walked down the stairs towards John's sparse office. When I entered, I found him slumped in his chair, staring out his window, looking rather depressed. Who could blame him? I knew exactly how he felt. John looked up at me and his first words were:

"I don't know what to do!"

53

This was not exactly what I wanted to hear. I was hoping that he had some great inspirational wisdom to share with me to strengthen my resolve for the hours and days to come. Having him basically mouth the very words I was feeling was deflating, to say the least. But what could I expect? No training can prepare you to deal with this type of tragedy. This wasn't just a normal death. It wasn't the end of a physical illness that we had all anticipated and for which we had prepared. No. This was far worse. This was murder! The taking of a life through violence leaves a far worst taste in your mouth then a so-called "normal" death. As perplexing as death can be, murder makes things even more confusing. There is no reasoning it through. No making sense of why it happened. No sense of being able to stop it if you tried. There is a *complete* helplessness and anger. I knew how John felt because I too was lost in a haze of confusion. I didn't know how to handle this tragedy either. However, my response surprised me:

"I don't know what to do either, **so let's do it anyway!**"

It emboldened me and became my private rallying call to action. It was such a simple yet profound statement, and I understood, deep in my soul, in those few confusing words, that it is okay to not know what to do.

It was a declaration of failure. Yet when I said it, I felt God leaping up within my soul in response to my words. It was as if this statement was exactly what God had been waiting for me to say so that He could have the freedom to take over. I would repeat it several times a day. These eleven words of confusing surrender and trust in God became my mantra. It inspired me to basically drop everything I was doing. I cleared my schedule, disappeared from my office and just hung out in the community, not knowing what to do other than just being present and available to God's work in me, through me and to the community around me.

I realized that this is what ministry is all about—not *knowing*, but just *doing*. It is this wonderful prayer of submissive action that God longs to hear from His children. It is only through these prayers of trustful surrender that our souls are emptied and consequently enabled to be opened for the infilling of God's Spirit. God's nearness to us can only be experienced when we get to the point in our lives where we sincerely ask Him to take over because we have no confidence in our own strength. Prayers of surrender, rendered from broken souls, have the spiritual power to unleash a person from any dependency on their own fleshly abilities. Surrendered souls are able and willing to be open vessels to be filled with God's power. The true essence of being a Christian is to surrender my agenda and to be present in the moment and available to God to use me any way He wants. In this way, He is freed up inside of me and His activity just *happens* all around me.

The result of this authentic openness to God was astounding. Complete strangers came to me to talk about spiritual matters, friendships of trust were developed, love was felt and spontaneous prayer meetings naturally occurred on street corners. True relational, down-to-earth, out-of-the-church-facility, on-the-streets ministry was happening because God's Spirit was active, filling my emptied surrendered soul with His presence, so that wherever I went, He was there. I was submitted to the Lord like never before. My agenda, strategies and dreams were replaced by God's presence. God moved through me to those around me, not because I am qualified or have any brilliant skills. I just made myself open and available to Him by admitting that I didn't know what to do. I was simply present and available to God and the community.

This needs to be the battle cry of every Christian: "I don't know what to do so let's do it anyway." Not having all the answers or skills to do ministry is a great thing to admit. Instead of letting our lack of ability or deficiency in knowledge stop us, it actually encourages us to go forth, totally trusting God for His skills and His words to do ministry. This is the way it should be. After all, it is **His** ministry, not **yours**. This is what walking by faith is all about. All those saints who were used mightily by God as mentioned in Hebrews 11 never had a seminary or university degree—but the one thing they all had in common was faith.

Faith is what made them successful because all they could do was trust that God would work through them. And He did. In 2 Corinthians 12:9, God says:

"…my power is made perfect in weakness." (NIV)

To admit we are weak and dependent on God is a wonderful thing. It is faith and it is this reliance on God that enables His power to perfect itself in our weakness.

It was in our weakness, in our grieving and tears that true soul-to-soul connecting occurred between us and the community of Warden Woods. We were joined together in our heartache over losing a beloved son in Patrick. We were one with them and when they saw us cry and deal with our sorrow, we were equals. This was when our ministry took off. We became one with the community, not because we had PhDs or effective urban training or exceptional skills. It was quite the opposite. We were effective because we were weak, broken and humble enough to just be present, warts and all. Something happened in the hearts of the people in Warden Woods when they saw our weakness, tears and pain. We were no longer outsiders who ran programs for their kids. Now we were one of them, crying tears just like them, for one of our fallen friends. There was a powerful connection made—a connection through grief and weakness.

In North America, we have not valued the incredible power of brokenness. In fact, we have despised weakness and made it a curse on our society. We expect our leaders to be strong, not broken people. Those in charge should have all the answers and possess no limitations. If you admit weakness, then you are putting your job and future in jeopardy.

Our worship of perfection has set us up for huge failures. This distorted view of perfect leadership often takes us away from depending on God for wise counsel. Instead of humbling ourselves and relying on God for His wisdom and strength, we place our trust in experts, books, conferences or educational training for the direction we need. We have shut the door on God's activity in our lives.

When brokenness is seen as a bad thing, we set ourselves up for a huge fall. Is it any wonder that in this culture of perfection many leaders struggle with hidden weaknesses and often end up in moral failure? It is hard for people in positions of leadership to admit their struggles when everyone, including themselves, have set themselves up to be flawless. Because of this, we lose the spiritual advantage of being weak and thus lose God's available resources to those who are humble. I love how *The Message* describes the power of brokenness and humility. In James 4:10, we read:

> "Get down on your knees before the Master; it's the only way you'll get on your feet."

The world needs broken leaders who are authentic people, with imperfections and scars, who are real before God and man. We need leaders who place more emphasis on trusting God than depending on man-made theories. I like what Henri Nouwen says about this in his wonderful book *The Wounded Healer*. To be a successful pastor, you must be authentic with those you serve. To be a healer, you must be genuine and vulnerable through your own wounds. In so doing, you become a wounded healer. God's healing touch to those who suffer can only go through people who are honest with their weaknesses and pain. The only ones who can be authentic healers to others must first be wounded themselves.

In the chapter entitled "Ministry For a Rootless Generation," Nouwen says:

> "We must be aware of the great temptation that will face the Christian minister of the future. Everywhere Christian leaders, men and women alike, have become increasingly aware of the need for more specific training and formation. This need is realistic, and the desire for more professionalism in the ministry is understandable. But the danger is that instead of becoming free to let the spirit grow, the future minister may entangle himself in the complications of his own assumed competence and use his specialism as an excuse to avoid the much more difficult task of being compassionate. More training and structure are just as necessary as more bread for the hungry. But just as bread given without love can bring war instead of peace, professionalism without compassion will turn forgiveness into a gimmick, and the kingdom to come into a blindfold."[1]

What is it that makes a person compassionate? Is it seminary training? A degree in psychology or an MBA? No. Compassionate people are those who understand what others go through simply because they are in touch with their own weaknesses and have embraced their own wounds. Compassionate people are broken people who have gone or are going through pain of their own and have owned this reality.

Sometimes the more education a person has, the more there is a temptation to see oneself above others. This creates a distance between a person and those being served. I prefer to have people who serve with me who are humble and dependent on God. I want people who have more questions than answers working alongside me. I want people who have a calling and a passion over those who have a degree and answers.

What qualifies a person to serve in God's kingdom is not their PhD but their broken spirit. As it is written in Isaiah 66:2:

"This is the one I esteem: he who is humble and contrite in spirit, and trembles at my word." (NIV)

Our society has become too institutionalized and professionalized. We are all starving for authentic community but are never fed. The church should be one place that is safe enough for us to let down our hair, share our burdens and receive the healing powers of grace and acceptance that God provides through His Body. I envision churches becoming more like Alcoholics Anonymous. Safe, healing places, full of hurting and broken people who enjoy gathering together with other hurting and broken people to worship the great Healer who Himself was acquainted with suffering. This is what James said the church should be like when he wrote:

"Are you hurting? Pray. Do you feel great? Sing. Are you sick? Call the church leaders together to pray and anoint you with oil in the name of the Master. Believing-prayer will heal you, and Jesus will put you on your feet. And if you've sinned, you'll be forgiven—healed inside and out. Make this your common practice: Confess your sins to each other and pray for each other so that you can live together whole and healed. The prayer of a person living right with God is something powerful to be reckoned with (James 5:13-16, The Message).

A few years ago, I had the joy of being involved in a church that lived out James 5:13–16. This church was full of young people who were a very hurting bunch, and every Thursday night they would come to their church in droves. The reason for this was quite simple. Thursday nights were a "no holds barred," free for all, worship service that was full of God's love and grace. Thursday nights were a time for troubled, hurting and broken youth to gather together and take off their masks in order to be real with God and one another.

Each Thursday night, this church would start out with our worship band usually rocking the place with some punk-infused worship song. It was a great band that I used to jokingly refer to as the world's most dangerous worship band simply because I did not know what would happen once they began to play. This hard-rocking, tattooed, ear, nose and lip pierced worship band consisted of a recovering heroin addict, a struggling marijuana user and a few other very interesting characters. Most of them had nicotine patches on their bodies to help them kick their cigarette habit and the majority of them were fairly new Christians. To the outsider looking in, the band must have seemed to be an unusual collection of characters, but I knew their hearts and how much they loved God. They would be the first to admit their struggles, but they did not make light of their personal challenges. Thus the nicotine patches on their skin. They were real about their faith and how God was transforming their lives one day at a time. No phoniness here, just real-life Christianity in action. I didn't mind their music style. They only knew how to play one way and that was loud. Yes, they were a unique bunch, but then again, this was a unique church and the worshippers that came on Thursday were an unusual group of people as well. They were the perfect fit.

When this band played, it was very common to see many people worship God with tears in their eyes as they were touched by the awesome love of their heavenly Father. At other times, they would dance for joy knowing how much He has done for them. It wasn't uncommon to hear new Christians share a testimony of what God was doing in their lives, laced with some profanity. This was okay with me, as they were sharing their hearts in its rawest form. A few of the youth who attended were pregnant teens, others were doing their community service with us because they had broken the law. Most did not know who their fathers were. The place was full of hurting people, and they were not afraid to admit it. No pride here, just brokenness and repentance, and I knew that God was smiling down on us!

This gathering of beat-up worshippers of God would often last three hours, and then we would all stick around afterwards for hours on end talking, praying or just having plain old-fashioned fun. Needless to say I ended up coming home at around 1:30 a.m. every single Friday morning because I had truly been at church. God was present every single Thursday night.

I end off with this story to illustrate the fact that it doesn't matter what type of church style is involved. The bottom line is that the church must be a safe place of love where hurting and broken people can come together, just as they are, and worship the great Healer. When this happens, God moves and His healing touch is felt through the music, the sharing, the Word and the Body of Christ, in the form of wounded healers.

---

[1] H. Nouwen, *The Wounded Healer*, Image Books, DoubleDay, New York, New York, 1972, p. 42.

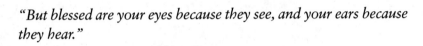

"But blessed are your eyes because they see, and your ears because they hear."

– Matthew 13:16 (NIV)

DO YOU SEE WHAT I SEE?

◆

CHAPTER FIVE

The day after Patrick's murder, I had the opportunity to be on a local talk radio station that bills itself as the nation's top-listened-to news station. I was a guest on their 7:00 p.m. call-in show as the result of the bloody evening the night before that left three men dead, one being our Patrick. The topic for the talk show was "Gang Violence in Our City," and I was asked to share my opinions with a live radio audience. The time was right to speak truth in response to the media that was abuzz with all sorts of negativity while racially profiling certain cultures in our city and targeting specific neighbourhoods. I had to give them a different message.

Before I accepted the invitation, I asked permission from Patrick's family. This was about him, not me, and I didn't want to do or say anything that would make them upset. I also invited them to join me if they wanted to.

They were too hurt to be on the radio, but they wanted me to be their voice and tell everyone how wonderful a young man Patrick was and to share with the city how great a neighbourhood Warden Woods is. This was a common theme from the people in the community. When Patrick's friends and other residents from the community heard that I was to be on the radio, many of them came and told me to speak out about Patrick and their community and to tell everyone to stop automatically blaming black youths for the crimes related to the gang spree happening in Toronto. I agreed wholeheartedly with them. My experience in the Warden Woods community was always positive. I felt that

I had a responsibility to open the eyes of some to see the good in our city and not just the bad. It was time to tell the truth about all the wonderful youth I knew at UrbanPromise.

Before I left for the radio station, I decided to bring Lucy Lee, our children's program director, and Vanessa, another of our excellent StreetLeaders. I knew that I wouldn't have all the answers, but with Lucy and Vanessa's help we would all be okay. I respected their wisdom and understood their hearts. They too had exceptional vision and compassion for what was truly happening in our city and they understood the real situation about our communities. They had "Jesus eyes" to see what was happening, and with them by my side I felt a unique power well up inside that I knew would keep me strong.

We were originally scheduled to be on the air for half an hour, but the show went so well and generated such a response that we ended up being on for an hour. I kept focused on the theme of all the good things happening in our city. I pointed to Patrick and the other youth at UrbanPromise as positive examples. I shared stories of how they were making a difference in the community. I scolded the media for profiling the negative elements present in our city instead of the positive. I talked about the many unsung heroes in our communities who are doing noble things that remain unseen because we do not put a spotlight on them. I mentioned that the media, inadvertently, are making gang life glamorous by always highlighting gangs. To me, this was irresponsible and it was time for the media to start highlighting the good instead of just the bad. My major thrust was to tell the city to stop judging young black males as criminals. This profiling was only making it worse for this segment of our population. To have to live with such a label was a hard cross to bear. Then, to prove my point, I said that most of the listeners out there, when they heard of Patrick, a young black male being shot in a gang-related murder, assumed that he was most likely a drug dealer or gang-banger just because of the colour of his skin. These comments I made about racial profiling had a special power simply because they were coming from a white man. No one could dismiss me or my words as coming from an angry, jaded, special interest group based on colour. The phone calls came in. We were on the hot seat for a long time, but the majority of callers were very positive and actually agreed with me. It was another moment when I thought how truly special my city is.

I love Toronto, the most multicultural city in the world, and most of those who called in that evening proved to be wonderful, accepting and caring people. It was clear that the listeners were able to see past the negative media portrayal as they voiced their opinions in support of what they heard from me about our communities and our people.

I also remembered other moments of goodness that occurred shortly after Patrick's murder. One day, while walking up the ramp into the Warden Woods Community Centre, I watched an elderly lady slowly make her way through a gauntlet of some pretty intimidating-looking youth. It was obvious that this woman was a stranger to the community. She had to be in her late seventies or early eighties and here she was, cane in hand, bravely ambling up the long walkway, past the media, right through the scary looking youth, into the community centre.

She went straight to the director and wrote out a cheque for Patrick's family to help pay for the funeral costs, saying, "When I heard the news I just had to do something to help. I hope this does."

Then she left. No one knew who she was and where she had came from. She was just a nice little old lady who had eyes to see and ears to hear what God wanted her to do for others. She understood the potential in the community and in the hearts of the youth who live there.

I received countless phone calls and e-mails from many friends as well as strangers. People wanted to help. They showed up in droves, bringing flowers, donating money or hanging around the community as support. They too were people who saw the good in our community. Too bad the media didn't report any of this.

Generally speaking, the church was magnificent through all of this. I was so proud to be a part of God's Church as it shone in great brilliance through this ordeal. I had so many pastors ask me what they could do to help. These were Christian leaders who saw perfectly the needs and opportunities that were present and wanted to do something practical. Many donated to funds to help cover the funeral expenses.

People responded in so many practical ways. Meals were provided to the family. Flowers were delivered to their door. Complete strangers were present and available with loving and compassionate actions. I was also amazed how the church community could be so easily mobilized. One church offered its large auditorium for free and then asked what else they could do. I told them that we were going to have a reception following the funeral and they volunteered to provide all the plates, cups and utensils. They also heard that I was going to rent buses to transport the people from the community to the funeral service and back because many of our people don't own a car. This church told me to save our money on bus rentals as they would also provide their church buses and drivers. Other churches provided food, drinks and money. Everything we needed was given. It was an incredible out-pouring of love. I was witnessing the willingness and power of a church ready to work for Jesus.

However, not all clergy were enthusiastic about providing practical loving support. Some pastors are unable to join with God in helping others because they are so consumed by their own agendas, a sad testimony for people who claim to be called by God to lead His flock. I was disappointed in some of these opportunistic individuals, who use people's misfortunes to draw the spotlight on their own ministries and personal egos. When tragedy struck, these pastors were using the opportunity to exploit it for their own purposes and recognition.

Some of these men, complete strangers to the family, came into the neighbourhood to visit with Patrick's family, but it quickly became apparent that they didn't have any concern for what the family was going through. They just wanted to use Patrick's murder to prop up their own causes. I actually sat in Patrick's living room and witnessed one of these pastors try to sell his anti-violence cause to Patrick's family. He was dressed immaculately and was a terrific speaker, but his words were condemning and misguided. He spoke how today's young people have no respect for the law and how this world is winning the battle of subverting our youth, especially through the vehicle of the public school system. Everything was negative and gloomy in his dark little world. Clearly he was blind to any form of goodness that was all around him. He presented his arguments in a well-rehearsed fashion based on the evils he saw in our city and was able to fluctuate his voice at all the right points for dramatic flare. This garnered a few "amens" from his assistant. It was a very manipulative presentation done simply to boost his manifesto, and when it was over, I was sickened and couldn't help but challenge him on his motives.

I personally disagreed with his solution to the problems in our city. His approach seemed to be a blurred vision—all talk and no action. He went on to blame and complain about the world, parents and our young people, and then wanted to protest all these problems via anti-violence rallies.

Complaining and holding rallies do nothing constructive for our communities, but they do get media attention and feed the ego of the organizer. Many pastors in the city regularly hold prayer marches, where they mobilize their congregations to be prayer warriors who roll into our communities and march about the streets in army fatigues, screaming out prayers and singing songs of praise and victory, while claiming the streets for Jesus. The media take the pictures, film the show and tape a clip from the pastor's motivational message to his troops and then show it in the late-night news, but nothing else happens. After a couple of hours of marching, singing and shouting, they leave the community exactly how they found it. Lots of sizzle, but few results.

I am so glad that Patrick's family saw through this pastor. After he made his sales pitch, one of the family members challenged him, asking if he had ever been in this community before. He replied he had not. Then Patrick's family said that before he could ever use their child as his project, he first needed to *be* here, working with the kids in practical ways, instead of keeping a safe distance away.

Pastors who parade around thinking that they are doing good things are mistaken. Those living in the communities where they march just watch from a distance, wondering to themselves what kind of strange thing they are witnessing. This achieves little success because these pastors are blinded by pride. The real tragedy is that when the marches are over and the last hot dog has been eaten from the anti-violence barbecue, they leave the community unaffected, only to return when another shooting occurs. They think they are making a difference, but all they really do is make a lot of noise, get a lot of press and further the stereotype of our communities as evil. They are just as bad as our blind and negative media, only seeing the bad and not the good.

Quite frankly, the people in our neighbourhoods are *embarrassed* by all the negative attention their community receives from these marches. It is tragic that they feel further stigmatized by the Church. Who can blame them when one prominent preacher declared to the press that his church would be holding a prayer march against the forces of evil in one of our communities and that if, by chance, he and his church members get shot while praying, then that was far better then having any more of their children dying from all the violence. The reality is that no one would ever get shot praying on the streets of our communities. But the sad thing is that his gifted speaking abilities were playing right into the hands of the media that pigeonhole our communities as bad places and thus stigmatize the people who live there as wicked. He is unknowingly labelling our people as evil. This is just an example of the negative rhetoric that gets this pastor great press but labels our people as violent and inferior. It curses our city.

If we are to pray against the violence in our cities then we need to do as Jesus tells us:

> "And when you pray, do not be like the hypocrites, for they love to pray standing in the synagogues and on the street corners to be seen by men. I tell you the truth, they have received their reward in full. But when you pray, go into your room, close the door and pray to your Father, who is unseen. Then your Father, who sees what is done in secret will reward you. And when you pray, do not keep on babbling like pagans, for they think they will be heard because of their many words. Do not be like them, for your Father knows what you need before you ask him" (Matthew 6:5-8, NIV).

Prayer was never intended to be used as a political form of protest. Yet, when I see some of these anti-violence rallies, I recall what Jesus describes above. Prayer and babbling on the street corners to be seen by many and broadcast to many more through the eyes of the media.

We as Christians have the power of God to bring healing to our cities. However, we must understand that this blessing power is not made manifest through methods of protest, marches and barbecues. The blessing will happen only when we pray with tears in our eyes in the privacy of our rooms and then go forth to serve our city. Then, instead of demonizing our institutions, we aggressively serve them and work with them to transform our cities. Jesus is into redemption not destruction. Our vision must be the same.

One of our staff at UrbanPromise always reminds those he works with to never forget to put on their "Jesus glasses." He knows very well that you can only see things properly through the eyes of Jesus. So every day we put on our "Jesus glasses" as we deal with the problems present in our city. We are positive and hopeful, believing that those we serve are full of God's glory. With this positive view in mind, we cannot help but have the right vision. We do it through practical acts of love and grace. We don't just see darkness and gloom, but understand clearly that the light always overcomes any form of darkness. Why curse the darkness when you can light a candle? Our approach is to roll up our sleeves, and instead of complaining about things like the public schools, we choose to work with them through our tutoring aspect in our after-school programs. We work with the people in the community, not as projects to be targeted, but as fellow friends who have the solutions.

We also teach our youth respect by first respecting them and allowing them opportunities to lead in their own communities through our StreetLeader program, to which Patrick was so dedicated. We tend to see the good over the bad and to flame the good into a fire of positive action that transform lives and communities. This is what Jesus did. He never met a hopeless case. In His eyes, everyone He met who had been written off by the ruling religious elite were not projects, but *potential*. This is why He never rejected anyone. His model must be our approach and that is to work together to "loose the bonds of wickedness" (Isaiah 58:6, KJV). He also called those He served to join Him in establishing the kingdom of God here on earth. This is what we try to emulate at UrbanPromise. We try to live out the Lord's Prayer as found in Matthew 6:10. We seek to establish God's kingdom come and His will be done in our city as it is in heaven. This means that we must be involved in justice issues, social concerns and good old-fashioned, practical, hands-on work as well as verbally sharing God's love with those around us.

In heaven, there is no racism, poverty, violence or injustice. Earth is our dress rehearsal for heaven and so we must be active in opposing these negative social concerns while we are here. We need to put on our Jesus glasses.

————————————◆————————————

"I will turn their mourning into gladness; I will give them comfort and joy instead of sorrow."

– Jeremiah 31:13 (NIV)

THE LEGACY OF PATRICK "DALTON" PITTERS

◆

CHAPTER SIX

As the days went by, I was able to spend more and more time with Patrick's family and I was asked to officiate the funeral. I now know why Patrick was such a great guy—he was the result of a wonderful family. We went to the funeral home and picked out a casket. It was blue, Patrick's favourite colour, and matched his camp nickname of "Blue Boy." We made the funeral arrangements and also booked a plot for his final resting place. We laid him to rest in the cemetery that was a close walk from his neighbourhood so his family and friends could easily visit him there.

When Patrick was first murdered, we were worried how the children and the youth would respond. Would there be a payback, a revenge killing, a "you killed someone from our neighbourhood so now we will kill someone from your neighbourhood" response? Often one murder leads to an escalation of violence as turf wars heat up.

Some youth were saying alarming things regarding their own futures. Despairing words were spoken:

"Why bother? Why even try to live life on the right path? Why even try finishing high school and go to college? Look at what happened to Patrick? He was the one that was going to make it. He was the one going places. He graduated high school and he was going to college and now he is dead. Why even bother? It is not worth it."

Back at the community centre, some of my staff took it upon themselves to plan a two-fold memorial. The first step was to make blue ribbons. They made hundreds of them for us to wear in honour of our "Blue Boy." Everyone on the streets of Warden Woods wore them, and it was comforting to see how many people loved Patrick. The second step was to make a large blank banner approximately 20 feet long and 4 feet wide. It was taped to a long wall in the centre and allowed people to write letters to Patrick and express their grief. It broke my heart to watch the children write notes to their hero, now in heaven. One young girl even wrote the following poem in honour of Patrick Dalton Pitters:

A Poem for Dalton

Dalton, sweet, quiet, and loves kids,
Brought many close, even kids.
He loved kids, I love him too,
And I'm sure many others do.
He was very great; known all over,
Never will be forgotten, ever.
I appreciate having him,
His light is never dim.
I thought of him as my brother,
He's like a warm, soft, comfy sweater.
Tears shed for him on the day he died,
We must be strong, we must not cry.
It hurt to see all those people cry,
But we look up at Dalton in the sky.

—Shannan Jones, 11 years old

These memorials had an incredible healing affect on the community, and in time the same youth that were so despondent immediately after Patrick's murder were now challenged to become like him. Through the memorial and the shared heartache of so many people, they understood how much Patrick was loved and respected by others. They saw how he had made such a huge difference in his community and now they wanted to be just like him. The same youth who once said, "Why bother?" were now telling us that they wanted to be like Patrick. They saw what his life had accomplished and that it was not a waste, but a tremendous legacy. They were now lining up to become StreetLeaders and to make a difference in their community, just like he did.

Patrick was a very simple God lover who touched so many lives. He was a young man of very few words, but a lot of patience, smiles and hugs. When he did speak, his words often carried the weight of great wisdom. A little boy he tutored in our after-school program told one of the most touching stories. One day, Patrick was helping him with his homework when the little boy asked: "Patrick, why are you so quiet? Why do you rarely speak?"

Patrick put his arms on the shoulder of the child, looked into his eyes and with a great big smile replied: "If I wasn't quiet, how would I ever hear you whenever you needed my help?"

I have a T-shirt that was made as a memorial to Patrick. On the front is his picture with the community as a backdrop and the words:

> *Dalton 'Blue Boy' Pitters R.I.P. Sunrise,*
> *July 17th 1984, Sunset, March 4, 2004*

and on the back:

> *Son, Brother, Uncle, Devoted, Loyal, Respectful, Caring,*
> *Beautiful, Humble, Legit, Quiet, Generous, Powerful,*
> *Responsible, Nice, Honest*

That is what he was to all who knew him, but he was also something else to our kids. In a community with very few fathers, Patrick was a surrogate dad to many of the children. To them, he was the only strong, positive male role model in their lives. And now he was gone. Forever.

The funeral was packed. More than 900 people attended and the service lasted over 3 hours. It was a triumphant going-away ceremony declaring to all that even in times of trouble and confusion, God is present. I was able to contain my tears as best as I could and preached what the Lord had placed on my heart. The entire ceremony was inspiring.

After the funeral, we had the committal at the graveside. It was a traditional Jamaican-style ceremony where we sang some old hymns and then everyone, individually, took turns with the shovel and threw dirt on the casket one by one. On the walk back to my car, I had many mourners come to me and ask what church I pastored. I could only tell them that though I was a pastor, I didn't pastor a specific church, but instead ran UrbanPromise Toronto. Then they said to me, "That's too bad because though I believe in God, I don't go to church but would if you were the pastor." One tall man with Rastafarian dreadlocks approached me and told me that my preaching touched his soul and that I was the only preacher he had ever heard who quoted rap artists in a sermon. He smiled a huge toothy grin and told me to keep it real. It was once again obvious that people are starving for God's truth when presented in an atmosphere of brokenness and grace.

We were then off to the community centre for a huge reception attended by at least 400 people. During this time, many more people approached me to ask where my church that I pastored was located. They, like my Rastafarian friend, were hungry for God and desired to find a safe community they could join to be a part of their journey through life. During the reception a petition was made up with people signing it. It was a request for me to start a church in the community centre for them. They were not kidding. I was surprised. Here I was, a white man, being beseeched by an all-black Caribbean community to start a church and lead them to God. That was unheard of—unchurched people, from a different culture, begging for a church in their community. This certainly put a twist on all the church-planting books and seminars that I had read and attended. But I learned something about ministry here. People are starving for God and are open to His servants who, in the words of my Rastafarian friend, *keep it real*. It doesn't matter the colour of their skin—that is just a barrier of the eyes. Love is colour-blind.

What really matters is that God's servants should just be there, hanging out without a clue what to do, but doing it anyhow. That is love incarnate in its rawest and purest form. We need to love and serve people by just hanging out. That is keeping it real. It may feel at times like we are doing nothing—just hanging around—but by physically **being there** we are doing something, because we are available. Hanging around for and with the dear people in that community *was* doing something.

I remember hearing about a pastor who was working on a sermon. He was busy writing his outline when he heard a knock at his door from someone who needed counsel. The pastor was upset that his valuable preparation time was being interrupted, and he quickly showed his unexpected guest how he felt. The guest quickly left without being able to share his heart. When the pastor went back to his study, he began to feel great shame. The Holy Spirit showed him that this guest was a divine interruption sent by the Spirit. The pastor repented of his sin and began to realize that ministry was a series of divine interruptions. Being available is a simple way to have God work His power through you into the lives of others.

Shortly after Patrick's funeral, I was asked to address a gathering of pastors at a luncheon. They had asked me to speak on how churches can impact their communities. I shared with them the theology of hanging out and told them that this is what Jesus did. I love what The Message says in its translation of John 1:14: "The Word became flesh and blood, and moved into the neighborhood."

Jesus' ministry was just to hang out with people. That was His divine strategy, and we too should follow it. I told the pastors, "For God so loved the world that He sent His son to 'hang out' with us."

I shared how Jesus' name, as found in Isaiah 7:14, is *Immanuel*, which in Hebrew means *God with us*, but could also be interpreted as *God hanging out with us*. He went to weddings, parties, walked the streets, ate at people's homes. In short, He hung out. His ministry came forth from hanging out with His Father and flowed into His ability to hang out with people. I then told them to be like Jesus and to just hang out in their communities. I informed them that their church could only impact their communities if they, as pastors, were serious about hanging out in their communities. They had to lead the way by looking into their day planners and start cutting back on their church appointments so they could spend at least half of their scheduled time open for divine interruptions by just hanging out in their communities. No agendas, no flashy programs, no hit-and-run excursions in and out of the community. Just be there. A loving presence in their community that is open to God and others. This way kingdom ministry will just happen.

Practical ideas were discussed, such as going to the nearby seniors' residence to hang out and play cards or checkers. In time, this would result in friendships developing, and with the integrity of true friendship comes divinely ordained opportunities to share and pray with the seniors. That is impacting their community. They would soon watch what God could do through them simply because they were available.

They were challenged to volunteer at the nearest community centre, public school or women's shelter.

Ministry isn't as hard as we make it to be. We have made it far too complicated. All we have to do is hang out with God and others. By making ourselves available, our preaching will come alive with real-life examples that, in time, will motivate others in our church to join us in hanging out in the community. We would now be leading a movement of hanging out. I ended my talk by declaring that it was time for us to have churches without walls.

The host of the luncheon came up to the podium and thanked me for coming. He then said that there would be a brief question period with the speaker. I soon discovered that my fine motivational speech of hope and inspiration didn't go as well as I thought. This group was divided into three camps. One camp seemed angry with me as I had threatened their comfortable ministry bubble. The other group was excited by my talk and raring to go into their community, and the third seemed indifferent as they rushed out at the end of my talk (and I assume they were not hurrying to leave in order to hang out in their communities.)

The questions were fired at me. One told me that my words were very optimistic but not realistic. He told me that his leadership board would never allow him to cut half his current schedule to spend time hanging out in his community. I asked him if his board had a passion to reach out to the community. He replied that they did, and to prove his point he shared how his board had just made up a new exciting vision statement for the church, reinforcing their great love for its community. Then I said, "If they have a passion to reach their community, they will let you take the time, even half of your weekly schedule, to be *in* the community. If they don't allow you to reprioritize your time, they do not have a heart for their community at all. If they oppose you, then they in fact are all talk and no action, because the truth of the matter is that we spend our time on things and with people we feel are important." Needless to say, he was not too happy with my words.

This ministry of hanging out should not be such a radical and disturbing challenge. In fact they are very basic, simple and practical ideas to apply. They are also based on solid Biblical truth. What pastor, with his or her schedule, cannot prioritize spending half of his or her time hanging out with people? Isn't that what pastors are supposed to do—

be with people? Pastors are also known as shepherds and shepherds spend time with sheep and even leave the 99 sheep to go out and find the one lost sheep (Luke 15:4). What shepherd doesn't hang out with sheep? What I was teaching wasn't a new paradigm of ministry, but in fact it was quite an old model. I was just re-affirming the old "parish model" that the Catholic Church used to apply. It is not a new strategy dreamed up by some radical urban missionary. It was a model of ministry exemplified by Jesus, who was always "hanging out" in the community. It has been tried, tested and proven.

I loved hanging out with Patrick's family and friends even at the after-funeral reception. The sound that came out of the community centre was loud and joyous. You wouldn't have known that this was a reception that had just followed a funeral. It was a real Jamaican party with dominoes, great island foods, drinks and lots of music and dancing. And there was I, in the midst of it all, just hanging out.

The highlight of the evening was watching the little children dance. They were incredible. While they danced and the adults watched, I snuck over to Patrick's mother and whispered in her ear:

"I will turn their mourning into gladness; I will give them comfort and joy instead of sorrow." (Jeremiah 31:13, NIV)

Patrick's mother smiled as she knew it was true. Though she had lost her son in such a horrific way, both God and Patrick had won. You can't kill a Christian. Our last breath on earth is our first breath in heaven. Patrick was now with his heavenly Father.

At the funeral, we showed a picture of Patrick taken on a trip with his UrbanPromise Toronto after-school kids to a farm in the country. In the picture, he is gently holding a lamb while smiling with delight. We added a caption to that picture with these words: "Now the Lamb of God is holding Patrick."

Much time has passed since the funeral and the police have yet to make an arrest. The longer this process drags on, the greater the chance that there will never be one. This is a hard case to crack. The ironic thing is that the reason the police are having so much difficulty in making an arrest is because they have no leads from Patrick's past. He had no shady connections for them to follow up on or cross-examine. They have made it clear that because Patrick had no criminal ties whatsoever and because none of his friends were involved in criminal activity, they cannot dig up anything to proceed with any leads. This is a testimony to Patrick's integrity as we await God's justice in His due time.

This was my first beautiful disappointment. To minister to that community, I had to experience their suffering first-hand. I had to allow myself the time and energy to be there, open and available to God's will for His hurting people. Through all the busyness of inner-city ministry, God could see how tired I was. He could also see what was ahead and already had me in the palm of His hand.

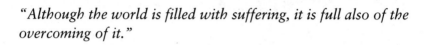

"Although the world is filled with suffering, it is full also of the overcoming of it."

– Helen Keller

HERE WE GO AGAIN

◆

CHAPTER SEVEN

I can't explain why bad things happen. It makes no sense to me at all. I especially can't understand why horrible things can happen to the same person in rapid-fire succession. But I do believe in hope, that God is present in the midst of everything, both good and bad. Yet knowing this does not diminish the fact that tragedies can significantly impact the flow of our lives. One way I try to make sense of it all is by seeing our lives as a beautiful sonnet written by God, the great Composer. I see life like one huge musical score containing various notes, crescendos, tempos and grooves. First, there are various rhythms found in the stages of our lives. All you have to do is think back over your own personal musical tastes while growing up to see the correlation that music has with your life.

Our development as human beings corresponds to music quite well. When you were a child, you had rhythm all over you and you could dance with the best of them. The musical score of your childhood should have contained lots of upbeat and happy grooves. To a child, life is meant to be an exciting dance. When you became a teenager, the music became more aggressive as you lived your life to the sound of a full-piece rock band or hip-hop rap crew. Rebellion was in the air and your developing mind became more critical of the things you accepted as a child. The loud music led to confusion, but in the midst of it all you believed that you were standing tall as your own person. As a young adult, the music morphed into a steady mixture of slow rock and R&B. You slowly became grounded in deeper responsibilities of family and profession and the rebellion of your youthful days became a lasting but fading memory. As you enter the senior years, the music slows down to a more mellow beat.

At times the score is slow, relaxing and peaceful, and at others a loud clash of cymbals interrupts your life and you are forced to deal with accumulating losses. However, because you have hopefully lived a long and productive life, you are able to bear the surprises of age with joy, dignity and hope. This is how life was meant to be lived.

During each of these stages, there is also a steady and growing rhythm of responsibility. Each stage consists of a system of living in which there seems to be a continuation of activity, friendships and duties. In each stage of our life we have routines. The alarm wakes us up in the morning and we begin our day, just like any other, with the same system in place of personal, familial and work or school-related functions. Each day is usually a continuation of the previous one, only to be interrupted every five days by a new rhyme called the weekend. Yet even this two-day break takes on a similar rhythm consisting of household duties, child sporting events and other typical weekend fare. When Sunday ends, the weekend rhythm is absorbed back into the same weekly groove that starts again every Monday.

These rhythms are not bad things. In fact, they can be positive as they provide a foundation for living upon which you can base your life. However, rhythms of life can be violently interrupted by tragedy and when this happens, life begins to unravel and not make sense anymore. All of a sudden, there is no rhythm or rhyme. The foundations crumble, the reliable system we have built around us comes to a halt, and we are left devastated.

This is what happened when Patrick died. The reliable rhythm of life no longer made any sense for the many impacted by his murder. Children could no longer dance, youths were made docile, young adults could no longer hope and even seniors were left without any peaceful wisdom for the circumstances. As for the daily rhythms of our lives—we were a mess. The alarm would go off in the morning and instead of awaking to the stability of responsibilities that awaited us, all we opened our eyes to was sorrow and confusion. Our regular daily functions seemed so unimportant and so stale in light of what had happened.

When faced head on with tragedy, nothing makes sense anymore. The rhythm of life becomes a jumbled distortion of chaos, confusion and pain, punctuated with hopelessness. The only rhythm one has in grief are regular outbursts of tears. But it is important to remember that these instances are either an anomaly to the music or, surprisingly, part of the score. In a fallen and sinful world, painful anomalies are inevitable. People will do evil things, we will make unwise choices and even natural disasters and sickness are all part of the results of the Fall. When sin is in the picture, nothing makes sense at all except for grace. The Composer of the universal song has written an original masterpiece that has been partially damaged and the results are obvious. The rhythms of life are sometimes disjointed by the results of our fallen world. However, all is not lost. The Composer responds to the anomalies and with tears in His eyes, is active in redeeming His song. In the end, He is able to make even the worst incongruities part of the score of our lives. Our trials and tragedies, placed within His masterful hands, will actually become the key notes of His musical masterpiece. To us it may not make any sense at all, but the Composer knows exactly what is happening, and in His hands all will work out in the end in a masterful "Hallelujah" chorus.

In time, life began to slowly make sense for us once again. A different rhythm gradually descended and Patrick's passing into glory served to make us all more mature, compassionate and strong. We were now living by a different beat—a new normal. There was finally a degree of peace and I could now allow time to heal from all the pain and confusion that I was enduring. However, little did I know that only five months later, I would have to endure yet another tragedy involving a child from Patrick's community.

On August 6, I received another one of those unforgettable phone calls. A staff person called my cell phone to inform me that there had been a terrible accident and one of our campers had drowned at an outing to the Toronto Beaches. The victim was an eight-year-old boy who was rushed to the hospital. At the time of the call, we did not have any current details about his condition. However, by all accounts, it didn't look good. When I heard the news, I was stunned. My heart stopped. It could not be true. This was my worst nightmare. The rhythm of life began to change once again. It was now up to the Composer.

As the executive director of an urban ministry, I had always had a concern about safety. This is especially so when it came to the children with whom we worked. This is only natural for any child or youth worker. Having the responsibility to oversee hundreds of children, youth and mothers always, without fail, gave me a degree of anxiety, especially when it came to children and water trips. Because of this we had developed strict water safety policies. We wanted to be able to have a tight rein on our kids, especially when they were in water. Safety was a priority, and our policies included many safeguards such as an extremely low camper-to-staff ratio that far exceeded the city's limits, staff involvement in all water activities where they were to be within arm's reach of each child in case of emergency, and updated first aid and CPR training for key camp leaders. We had done all we could to make water safety a priority but, as I was later to discover, an accident can still happen as it did on that cool August afternoon.

When I received the call, I didn't know the name of the child or if he were even alive. However, I was told the camp name, and when I heard that, my heart broke. It was Camp Hope.

UrbanPromise Toronto operates various summer day camps in the city. Each camp has a different name based on hopeful dreams for the future. Names like Camp Hope, Peace, Victory, Freedom, Joy, etc. Camp Hope was the same camp, staff, children and community that had just suffered Patrick's loss! I was stunned. This was unreal. It was bad enough that we had to deal with this drowning, but what was even worse was that it involved the same people who were still dealing with their own grief over Patrick. I was struggling to believe that this could be happening all over again. I raced home, got changed and then rushed off to the Warden Woods Community Centre. *Lord, why would this happen there again?*

On the way to the centre, I remembered many of the lessons I learned throughout Patrick's ordeal. Once again, this was something for which no one ever can prepare you. These types of trials are not things that you can be trained to handle. They are just tragedies you hope to avoid. The first thing I needed to do was to check in with my staff to see how they were holding up before I went to the hospital to be with this precious child and his family. When I got to the community centre, my staff was in a state of shock and intense grief. Most were just staring glazed eyed into nothingness, crying on each other's shoulders or praying in small groups. Who could blame them? They had all just gone through a horrible ordeal. I quickly gathered them together, did a quick debrief on what had happened, and had one of my staff who was not from this camp make sure each staff person from Camp Hope wrote out incident reports. I ended my quick meeting by telling them that I loved them, and then finished off in a time of group prayer, asking God to spare the young boy's life and comfort his family as well as our staff and the community. That night, most of the Camp Hope staff did not want to be alone, so they spent the weekend together at the home of one of their camp directors.

Then I went to the hospital with great fear and trepidation. I was scared of the unknown. I didn't know what to expect when I got there. My mind was bombarded with many questions, great concerns and prayers for the well-being of this little boy. *Was he still alive?*

I prayed for a miracle and even reminded God that He owed us one after what we had just been through with Patrick's murder. Surely He could bring healing. No, surely He *would* bring healing to this child and we would have a triumphant story to tell. After all, God can perform miracles, and in all fairness, if ever a group of people deserved one, it was us and it was now! I also wondered how the parents would react when they saw me. This was an obviously excruciating time for the family. I wept for them. I knew that I also had to deal with the media already leaving messages at my office, hounding me on my cell phone, stalking me for a response. All of these thoughts, fears and concerns filled my head, but I couldn't dwell on these issues. My only concern was to get to the hospital as fast as possible and do all I could to help this child and his family get through this trial. In my heart, I prayed and prayed that God would perform a miracle and all would be well.

The good news was that the little boy was alive and fighting for his life in the hospital. He was a beautiful child with a smile that lit up the room, always happy, encouraging and full of energy. He kept all of us on our toes as his energetic curiosity often had him off running, away from the group, experiencing his own adventure. This boy lived life with passion and abandon. He danced the rhythm of his life with great vigour and joy. Everywhere he went, positive energy followed him. He was fast, inquisitive and a whole lot of fun. He never got into fights and never back-talked his leaders. He was a well-mannered, respectful, optimistic bundle of joy. He was famous for phoning his favourite camp counsellors throughout the year, to talk and to see how their day had been. It was amazing to see how a little guy like this touched so many lives.

When I got to the Hospital for Sick Children, I was relieved to see that Michelle, our director of counselling, was already there with the child's mother. Michelle was at the camp when this wonderful mother first found out what had happened and accompanied her in the police cruiser all the way to the hospital. To me, Michelle is a modern-day version of Mother Teresa, a godly woman with a huge heart for God and others. She has the ability to calmly deal with high levels of stress with a constant smile and a peaceful air about her. When she speaks to others, you sense God's peace in her words and actions. I was so glad to see her there. I wasn't alone in that hospital, and she was someone I could lean on during those first few days there. Only later, after I told Michelle how her presence was such a great encouragement to me, did I find out that she felt the same way about having me there. We needed each other to lean on for strength.

I was rushed up the elevator to be with the worried mother who was waiting for any shred of news. I entered the private waiting room where she nervously sat in a chair and identified myself to her. I expected her to get angry with me for this horrible accident. During the drive to the hospital, I had prepared my soul to be crushed. In my heart I could never blame her if she were upset. Though I wasn't at the beach that day, I was the executive director of UrbanPromise. I had started this ministry and it was my program that was involved with her child when the accident took place. Because of this, I always have felt a great deal of responsibility for whatever happens, good or bad, in UrbanPromise. With a heavy and worried heart, I entered the room and approached the lone figure sitting in the drab chairs of your typical hospital waiting room. There she was, a mother awaiting news from the doctors regarding the well being of her son. As our eyes connected, we hugged. I was surprised by her grace and acceptance. Blame was not her manner. She was the perfect picture of peace and grace under fire and remained this way throughout the ordeal.

I am forever grateful for the way she handled this tragedy. It may sound hard to believe, but I forget what I initially said to her when we first met. But what rests with me is how together we talked, waited and prayed. A friend of the family who was a real support throughout this ordeal later joined us. She was a very positive person to have there as her presence and faith were a tremendous pillar of strength for all of us in the months to come. That night, we kept vigil until the early hours of the morning. We ended up doing this for over two months.

The next day, I addressed the media and let them know what was happening. I was in tears trying to describe how my staff and I felt since we deeply love the kids and families we serve. I ended the interviews asking people to pray for this little boy's recovery. He was one of our own, a wonderful child, and we were all left brokenhearted. This grieving was all the more difficult as it occurred right on the heels of Patrick's death. This was our second tragedy in five months.

Later in the day, I went back to the hospital and was able to meet with the little boy's father. What a tremendous encouragement he was to me. He proved to be a wonderful man of great faith who earlier that day had amazed the media by telling them that he held no blame or anger towards the UrbanPromise staff, and that he felt horrible for what we were going through. I was deeply touched as he mentioned to the press that he was praying for us, just as we were praying for him.

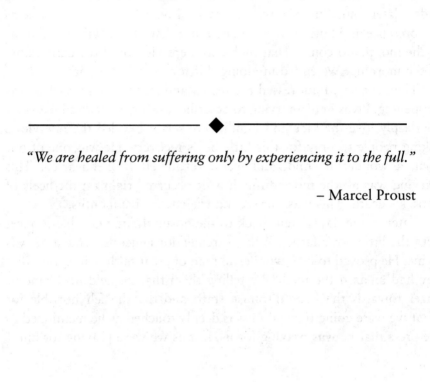

"We are healed from suffering only by experiencing it to the full."

– Marcel Proust

DON'T RUN AWAY—RUN TO

◆

CHAPTER EIGHT

One of the many things I learned during this time of dealing with deep pain, loss and trials was that when tragedy strikes, no matter how "together" we seem, our natural instinct is to run away from the problem. This desire to flee increases according to the depth of pain and trauma we are enduring. For all of us who were intimately affected by these losses, each day was a sorrowful discipline of getting out of bed to face another day of sadness. For me, it involved comforting a grieving family, my staff, an entire community and my own hurting heart. I am sure that everyone involved felt the same way. We fell asleep sad, but by sleeping we were provided an escape, a much-needed break from the pain endured, only to have to wake up right back in the middle of the problem. I was now a personal friend of soul trauma. I was slowly coming undone.

In light of all the confusion, fear and grief with which I was dealing, I sought out other leaders who had gone through similar experiences. I began to make some phone calls and asked around to see if there were any others who had been through similar tragedies. I needed someone I could speak to, somebody who would understand what I was going through. I desperately needed to know if there was hope and an end to the pain. To my surprise, I couldn't find anyone. However, there were a few close leads. I remembered some friends telling me about a camp director who had also experienced a drowning in his own pool. When I asked for this person's name, I was told he had quit right after the accident because the pressure got to him. No one knew where he was, so I could not get a hold of him.

Another friend mentioned someone who ran a ministry that experienced a somewhat similar tragedy. One of their vans had an accident, killing some staff and young people who were in the vehicle. However, this person had also resigned from his position shortly after. I couldn't find a single person who was available to talk to me about what I was going through because they had all quit! It was a terribly lonely experience. Inside my soul I was fragile and broken, and outside things were even worse! All around me buzzed a chaotic whirl of sorrow that I felt needed to be addressed by my pastoral help. However, it was hard to be supportive when my own soul was in need of support itself.

One person who was very helpful to me during this second crisis was my brother-in-law who works as a search-and-rescue technician (SARTEC) for the Canadian Armed Forces. His job puts him directly into crisis after crisis, dealing with tragedies such as sinking ships and plane crashes. In his line of duty, he is forced into traumatic circumstances where he is relied upon to save many lives. However, there have also been times when he has lost people. He knows what it is like to suffer loss and has, due to his vast experience, become a counsellor for other SARTECs who have gone through similar trauma. I really appreciated his casual way of providing help. He would call me to see how I was doing, and was skilled in asking the right questions to get me to voice what I was feeling inside.

Having someone to talk with, who knew exactly what I was going through, was a great help. One comment that stuck in my mind as a key turning point occurred while we were walking down a lazy country road in his hometown. As we walked and I talked, he made a startling statement. He told me that over 80 percent of all leaders will quit after they experience a tragedy, even if they were not directly responsible for what had happened. I knew that this was me. In other words, there was an 80 percent chance that I would pack it in and leave UrbanPromise. I have to admit that the thought of quitting had crossed my mind countless times during this second tragedy. *Why not? Why bother putting up with this pressure? I could just run away like all the others.* I was now going through my second traumatic experience in such a short time. Enough was enough! *If most people quit after one tragedy, surely I was justified in quitting after two in a five-month period. Why drag my family through all of this again?* I basically had to fight my way through all of the pressures and stress, trial after trial, and deal with the ultimate question staring me in the face—*Was all of this worth it?*

My brother-in-law's statement opened the door for further conversation, and I was able to slowly work out my feelings regarding my strong desire to drop everything and give up. I decided to buck the odds and instead of choosing flight, I decided to fight. Fight my fear. Fight my pain. Fight the spiritual chains that seemed to hold me down. Fight to survive by walking through the valley of the shadow of death, clinging to my Good Shepherd who will, in His time, lead me to a banquet table (Psalm 23). To flee would mean never dealing with the loss. To abandon the course that I was now walking would only result in deeper spiritual, emotional, psychological and physical hardships. I knew that to give up now meant that I would be like all the others who quit before me and are now suffering worse pain then ever because they never dealt with their tragedy. To leave now would mean that I would always be haunted. I decided to fight to live. I decided to stay the course.

I learned some very important lessons through Patrick's death that I was able to apply here. I learned that when you go through a hard time, it is important to fully process it. By asking the right questions, in the midst of what I was going through, I was able to *own* my feelings, fears and problems. By facing the pain, I was able to cry deeply in my soul about what had happened. This allowed me to be emotional and angry with God and my friends. I became an open book while going through everything, and because of this, I received healing from God through His words spoken in the deepest places in my soul and through His people.

My family was a tremendous source of strength to me. My wife Judith, as she has always been, was right there with me throughout this whole ordeal. In fact, she was very involved in caring both for our grieving staff and the family who was now mourning the loss of their young son. Judith was by my side on a daily basis as we visited our little camper at the Hospital For Sick Children. My staff, as usual, was also a source of mutual strength. I was not alone—we were all in this together.

I felt the Lord telling me that His presence was right here with all of us. In fact, that presence was in the very thing I feared the most. God was in the hospital, right there with the little boy fighting for his life, and He was there with his family. There was no way that I was going to abandon them, as I knew that if I ran away from them, I was running away from God. It was as if He were telling me not to run *away* from problems but to run *right to* them and embrace them. By doing this, I would encounter God in a fresh way and in a new light. The reality is that if I ran away, I would never be able to recover personally. By running from problems, we only allow them more control.

Our problems live within. When you go through a traumatic experience, it digs deep into your soul. It sets up shop inside your spirit. It becomes a part of who you are. Therefore, you must accept the reality that it is there. If you don't embrace the trial and instead try to sweep it under the carpet, or try to run away from the reality, then the tragedy will begin to show up and control you in negative ways. This is why people suffer through physical, emotional, psychological and spiritual illnesses. Avoidance leads to suffering.

Depression, physical health issues and an immature faith are only some of the symptoms that can raise their ugly heads inside you if you try to run. You can only attempt to ignore the obvious for so long until deeper problems settle in. Each of these symptoms are signs that you have issues inside your soul that need to be dealt with. I realized this as I went through this second tragedy and it was then I decided to fully embrace it. I knew this meant that one of my responses had to be to prioritize my time—to be present in that hospital with this little boy and his family.

Paul, who was very familiar with suffering, writes to young Timothy to prepare him for the inevitability of trials he will undoubtedly face. His advice is simple. Timothy is not to run away from hardships and pain but to "depend on God." Paul says:

> "For God did not give us a spirit of timidity, but a spirit of power, of love and of self-discipline." (2 Timothy 1:7, NIV)

Timidity is the same as fear. It is the fear of not knowing what to do, what to say or how to react. Timidity can paralyze you from taking action. It makes you stay put instead of moving you forward, and it will block our access to the Spirit of His power, love and self-discipline. To cave in to timidity is basically sinful disobedience! To run away is to not trust God but to believe instead that God has abandoned you. For me to run from the tragedy I was now facing was to say that God was too weak to deal with my problem.

This spirit of fear is not from God. To run away from a problem is to obey another spirit, rather than depend and rely on the true Spirit of God. If we quit due to fear, we are disobeying God because we refuse to trust His Spirit, given to us, this promised Spirit of power, love and self-discipline.

I can honestly say it wasn't easy, but I am glad I was able to trust God. He gave me the strength to overcome my fear and allowed me to rely on the Spirit of love to spend time with this little boy and his family throughout that ordeal. I also depended on God to give me the Spirit of self-discipline to set aside time, stare the problem right in the face and not run away. I had to stay put and walk through this with the family. I was glad I did. With our minds made up to stay the course, Judith and I had the privilege of spending long hours in the hospital. We did it in shifts, trying to spend every day there as a support to the family. We quickly came to love them as we were drawn closer through the tragedy.

At first, our motivation behind these visits was to comfort them, but in the end we received far more comfort from them then we could ever give back. I am still in awe when I think back to how this family responded to this tragedy. They were a tremendous source of strength to everyone around them.

With the many prayers of our staff, friends, this family and the ever-present prayers of the little boy's grandmother, we were all able to keep going strong. Both parents touched our hearts deeply. Our staff, Judith and I spent weeks in tears, prayer, worship and much time fasting throughout the entire ordeal. Looking back, I now know that we did the right thing by walking through this ordeal together. If we had quit and ran away, we would never have experienced the healing that God gave us through being together. God was moving among us and though we still don't understand why these types of things happen, we *do* know that God was with us, every step of the way.

This precious little boy clung to life for over two months at the Hospital for Sick Children in Toronto. His wonderful, supportive and loving family was always present, visiting him with his mother constantly by his side. All through this time, my wife and I were able to invest most of our time to be with the family. This little boy was one of our UrbanPromise kids, and his family was also one of our families. One of our own was hurting, and because of this we also hurt. During the countless hours in the hospital, I was able to strike up a wonderful friendship with the father, who was rooted in our faith. I still can see his face light up and hear his warm voice tell me how much he loves his heavenly Father. It wasn't just a statement, but a heartfelt, sincere burst of praise. I learned so much from him.

Eventually, this little lad succumbed to brain damage as a result of the drowning. Once again, we were all devastated. God did not do what we wanted Him to do. There was no miracle. A healing was not in the books. Yet God was with us once again. In the pain and our tears, there was an unexplainable presence of hope. Reflecting on the life and death of his little camper, one of our summer camp counsellors, a StreetLeader from his community, wrote this rap song about him and the influence of his young life:

Thumpz—Rest In Peace

Now That You Gone It's An Issue
It's Like My Visual Still Here But My Soul Gone With You
My Body Feels Empty, Piece Of My Heart Is Missing
You Helped Me Build The Man Inside Of Me And How To Listen

Losing A Young Strong Man Like You Is A shame
But These Tears We Cry Bring Laugher, Joy And Pain
The Camp Hours, I Was Your Father, You Were My Son
The Devil Knew You Were A Threat To Him, So He Fought The Lord And Won

Your Life Hasn't Begun And You Are Over The Clouds
You May Be In A Better Place But Why You Have To Go Now?
What You Mean To Me, Words Can't Even Explain
I Wish Somehow My Life And Your Life Could Be Exchanged

If It Could Be Arranged, I'd Be Up There Trust Me
Lookin' Down, Seein' you Growin' Up, Watchin' You Succeed
In My Heart Is Where You'll Be Forever, Friend
One Day Not Just Me, But We'll All Be Together Again

Chorus:

Too Bad You Couldn't Ride Any Longer
Went To Your Funeral, Seen A Smile On Your Face,
You Died In Honour
Everyone Cryin', Every Race Was Hurt
I Know You Still Livin', But Not On The Face Of The Earth .
You Put A Big Smile On Everyone's Face When You Were Around Us
You Still Are But Now You're A Great Angel That Surrounds Us
I Remember It Like It Was Yesterday, We Had The Pillow Fight
You Changed Everyone's life, During Your Little Life

You Always Came To Me First For Help
Me And You Tak'in Other Opponents, That Was Great And Them
Other Moments
Them Times When You Were Walkin' Wit Me
Look In The Clouds, I Can See Your Face, I Can Hear You Talkin'
To Me

All Them Other Kids Shined But You Really Stood Out
And When I Was Mad Or Down You Brought The Good Out
You Were Like My Own Son Plus A Brother Too
You're Special And There'll Neva Be Another You

Chorus:

A Lot Of People Want To Be Just Like You
When I Have A Son, I Want Him To Grow Up And Be Just Like You
When You Came Into This World, You Had A Special Gift
No One Has It Thug, We Still Don't Know What It Was

I Sometimes Get Mad At God Cause He Took You Out Son
But He Spoke To Me And Told Me It's Better In The Outcome
Cause You Aint Gotta Worry About Guns And Bad Stuff
And People Hatin' On You Or G'ttin' Put In Handcuffs

But By Your Style And Personality, You Wouldn't Be In It
You'd Have A Good Job, Life So Hard
We Luv You, And That'll Never Be Taken Away
It's A Shame That Everyday People Being Breakin' Away

When Funny Things Used To Happen You Were Laughing With Me
We One, Whatever Happens To You Happens To Me
If Anyone Asks, Who Made A Diffrence In My Life, I Say You
I Thought This Be The Last Thing I'd Say, Rest In Peace

– Written by Jordan Thoms

Patrick's murder and now the loss of this little life through a drowning—both unexpected tragedies and both occurring within five months. After this second funeral in such a short time span, I knew I had hit the bottom physically, emotionally and even spiritually. I was out of gas. There was nothing left in the tank. I knew that I needed to get away, with my family, on a sabbatical where I could gain perspective and be restored by God.

This was not just something that I needed personally. There was also a great need for my family to be with me and experience a long period of undisturbed renewal. My wife and I had been so busy dealing with so much tragedy that our children now needed us all to themselves. They were suffering, just like we were, and were exhibiting signs of childhood stress. Now, finally, restoration was on the menu. At last we could get away and be renewed. At least that was what we thought. But once again, we were about to embark on another trial. This time it involved us on an even more personal level.

―――――――――――◆―――――――――――

"Before we can pray, 'Lord, Thy Kingdom come,' we must be willing to pray, 'My Kingdom go.'"

– Alan Redpath

THE PRAYER OF OPEN HANDS

◆

CHAPTER NINE

In light of the two tragedies that had happened so close together, I recognized my need for some personal healing. I was a mess, and my family was hurting as well. With lots of questions and no answers, I approached my board of directors and requested a sabbatical break. The purpose of this time away was for us to experience a brief respite from the storms of urban ministry. We desperately needed to get some space where we could wait on God and allow Him to deal with the hurt and confusion that was present in our souls. It was obvious to the board that the unprecedented pressure in serving broken-hearted people, while also dealing with my own grief, had taken a heavy toll on its executive director and his family. They granted permission for my family and I to have an unmitigated time of rest, rejuvenation and restoration.

Deep in my soul, I just knew I had to go. In fact, the only thing that kept me stable throughout the last ordeal of watching this little boy slowly slip into eternity was the strong conviction I had that God was telling me to wait it out and that when it was over, He would meet with me in a special way through a sabbatical rest. So, when the funeral was over, I felt the Lord release me to get away and spend extended time with Him. I also felt He would reveal Himself to me in a very special and intimate way. I naïvely thought that the worst was over. The time had finally come for my family and I to be released and to go away for a time of restorative peace. My board had given me a green light, and I was ready to leave my worries and concerns behind me.

As we planned our three-month getaway, my wife Judith and I wanted to make sure that we would get the most out of our sabbatical rest. We decided to meet regularly with a very wise friend of ours who was a gifted spiritual director. Our time with her was valuable in preparing us to get the most out of our sabbatical encounter with God. During our times together, we were directed to read certain books, pray certain prayers and read particular Scriptures. During our last session, just days before we were to leave, she challenged us to do something that was very hard for both of us. She asked us to pray the prayer of "open hands."

The open-handed prayer is an ancient form of prayer where you pray to God with the backs of your hands resting on your knees while your palms lie open. This prayer is a symbol to God that what you are praying is done in a spirit of surrender. A prayer with open hands is proclaiming to God, "Your will be done in my life, whatever that will may be."

We were asked to surrender our sabbatical to God and trust Him to lead us in any way He wanted. We struggled with this one. *How could we do this after what we had just gone through? Where was God when Patrick was murdered? Why doesn't He protect children from drowning accidents?* We were scared and worried about what was coming next. A murder, a drowning and then what? Our lives seemed to be one giant case of bad news that just got worse and worse.

Though these fearful doubts were present, we were able to balance our worries with the ever-increasing intimacy we experienced with God in the midst of the past months. It was strange and mysterious how close God's presence was to us in the midst of our pain. There was no natural explanation for the peace and comfort we received amidst our tears throughout the confusing ordeals we went through. Though we still didn't understand why these terrible things happen, we nevertheless experienced God's love in the midst of the tragedies. We knew He was present with us through it all.

God is unpredictable. In the C.S. Lewis classic *The Lion, The Witch and the Wardrobe*, we come across what I consider to be an incredible description of Jesus. Many of us are familiar with this story, in which four children are transported through a magical wardrobe closet into a strange new land inhabited by all sorts of unique creatures, including talking animals. This land of magic is called Narnia. Unfortunately, it faces a never-ending winter due to the wicked spell placed on it by the evil White Witch, who is able to turn to stone any creature she touches. In fear of her dark powers, many creatures have joined her in her evil crusade of destroying anyone who opposes her rebellious and dark ways. This witch obviously symbolizes Satan and those who stand with her represent his minions. Rising up against her is a small band of animals and creatures led by Aslan, an all-powerful lion who has just returned from an extended absence. Aslan is the perfect representative of the Lion of Judah, Jesus Christ, and those who stand with Aslan are the angels of heaven.

Instrumental in the defeat of the wicked witch are four children who have stumbled into Narnia via the magical wardrobe. The two boys are referred to as the "Sons of Adam" and the two girls are known as "Daughters of Eve." As humans, they are held in highest honour by Aslan and his army, and because of this, they are regarded with the greatest contempt by the witch and her forces. Lewis brilliantly uses his story to clearly describe the spiritual battle between God and Satan, good and bad, right and wrong. It is a struggle for the hearts of mankind. In the end, Aslan triumphs after using an incredible strategy in which he gives himself up to die under the hands of the witch, and later raises from the dead to defeat her—a wonderful description of the death and resurrection of Christ.

The first time the children hear about Aslan is when they stumble across two lovable talking beavers. During their conversation, Lucy, one of the daughters of Eve, curiously asks the hospitable beavers some questions about Aslan. This is the most powerful description of Christ that I have ever read:

"But shall we see him?" asked Susan.
"Why, Daughter of Eve, that's why I brought you here for. I'm to lead you where you shall meet him," said Mr. Beaver.
"Is—is he a man?" asked Lucy.
*"Aslan a man!" said Mr. Beaver sternly. "Certainly not. I tell you he is the King of the wood and the son of the great Emperor-beyond-the-Sea. Don't you know who is the King of the Beasts? Aslan is a lion—**the** Lion, the great Lion."*
"Ooh!" said Susan, "I'd thought he was a man. Is he—quite safe?

I shall feel rather nervous about meeting a lion."
"That you will, dearie, and no mistake," said Mrs. Beaver. "If there's anyone who can appear before Aslan without their knees knocking, they're either braver than most or else just silly."
"Then he isn't safe?" said Lucy.
"Safe?" said Mr. Beaver, "don't you hear what Mrs. Beaver tells you? **Who said anything about safe? 'Course he isn't safe. But he's good. He's the King, I tell you."**[1]

Lewis wrote this story to vividly explain that life is an unravelling story of the battle between good and evil, and the triumph of good over evil through the presence of the kingdom of God. But this battle of history is not just between God and Satan. It also involves nature and humanity. We all play a part as children of Adam and Eve. Because of this, life can seem very confusing, especially when evil seems to triumph.

However, one thing we can depend on is this: Jesus is the King and He is good. We must also understand that He cannot be tamed—He is good, but definitely not safe. And it is this unpredictable reality of God, this "unsafe" quality of Christ, that makes life both confusing but also an adventure. Personally, I wouldn't have it any other way.

People have tried to tame the Lion, the King, God. This has caused our faith to be a predictable life of boring routine instead of an exciting adventure. We have tried to de-claw the lion and make God safe through "feel good" theology (as if we could neatly put God and His ways into a neat formula), "don't rock the boat" churches, comforting music and some weak-kneed books. We have gone to great pharisaical lengths to control the Lion that cannot be tamed! I know this because I have been part of trying to analyze the living God, the Holy of Holies, the Lion of Judah, and I discovered the hard way. He will not bow down to my theories, theology and comforting philosophy—He refuses to be tamed! In the midst of our attempts to control Him, something unsafe happens. Something rocks our world over which we have no control. An illness in the family, the death of a loved one, the deception of a spouse or close friend, an unexplainable tragedy. All of a sudden, all the theories we teach and have been taught, all the books we have read and all the conferences we have attended have no answers to what is happening in our world. Something horrible has happened; confusion reigns and our views about God and His plans are challenged.

The man-made formulaic foundation upon which we have built our lives, ministries and businesses has been shifted with earthquake-like proportion and we are left standing alone with nothing—no answers, no advice, no gurus, nothing. Yet in the distance, I hear the Lion roar, and though we are left dazed and confused by our horrible circumstances, Aslan is on the move!

We all will experience at some point the crumbling of our self-importance through the trials of life. Life's struggles often remind us how weak we truly are and how much control we lack. My safe, deceptive life of control was devastated like never before through these two tragic experiences, and when your world falls apart, you then realize what the daughters of Eve were told,

"Safe...Who said anything about safe? 'Cause he isn't safe. But he is good. He's the king, I tell you."

He is the King, and you are not. We need to stop acting like we have everything under control, because life teaches us that we can control nothing.

So now here we were, Judith and I, wrestling with our fears after being invited to pray the prayer of open hands before this wonderful, unsafe, but always *good* Lion.

Slowly, with our hearts racing in unison, we lowered our arms, rested our hands open on our laps and told God, with tears in our eyes, to have His way with us. Did we really have a choice? Little did we know that in a few days this prayer would come back to us in a powerful, life-changing way.

---

1 C.S Lewis, *The Lion, The Witch and the Wardrobe*, HarperCollins Publishers Ltd., London: 1950. p.75.

---◆---

"Maui No Ka 'Oi"

– Maui is the best

SABBATICAL UNREST IN HAWAII

◆

CHAPTER TEN

Our sabbatical began as we got off the plane after touching down on the runway at Kahului Airport with a sign greeting us "Welcome To Maui." There was really no need for a sign to welcome us to this beautiful island as the hospitality of the "aloha" spirit permeated everything around us. The feel of the warm tropical air on the skin said, "Aloha." The smiling faces of all those around us declared, "Aloha." The chirping of the birds in the blue cloudless skies sang out, "Aloha." Even the very ground we walked on shone brightly as it reflected the clear sunlight like a flashing neon sign. *Aloha. Welcome to Maui indeed.*

"Maui No Ka 'Oi" is a common phrase that the locals love to say. It means Maui is the best, and it is hard to argue with them on this point. On that November day, with all of the stresses of ministry left behind, Maui truly seemed, at least to me, to be heaven on earth.

It was here in this island paradise that my family and I began our trip of a lifetime. The adventure began right after we picked up our rental car and started out on a dawdling drive along a stretch of highway famously known as the road to Hana. This stretch of road bobs and weaves along the Maui coastline, in and out of the flowering rainforest, with dangerous ocean cliffs beckoning inches from the side of your car. It is only about fifty miles long, but it takes over two hours to get from one end to the other.

There are many reasons why your car travels at sloth-like speeds on this wonderful thoroughfare. The most obvious one is that you cannot help but drive slowly when you have so much incredibly beautiful scenery along the route. Every mile is jam-packed with picture-postcard moments of gorgeous waterfalls, flowers, rain forests and crashing waves dancing on the rocky crags of the sandy beaches below. The breathtaking views demand that you drive slowly so you do not miss one of the many stunning sights that envelop your car. Many times you cannot help but fall into the temptation of nature's dazzling call and you have no other option but to pull your car over to the side of the road for many scenic breaks.

Also, with over 600 hairpin turns and 54 one-lane bridges, you are forced to drive slowly! Since these bridges only allow one car to travel on them at a time, you have to slow down even more in case you need to let an approaching car cross the bridge. Though this forced, slow-paced driving would seemingly bother most city slickers, the scenery will cause even the greatest, lead-footed speed demon to miraculously transform into an ear-to-ear grinning Sunday driver. It is for good reason that this stretch of highway carries the title as the most beautiful road in the world. One can hardly be faulted for having a bad case of rubber necking while driving this patch of magnificent asphalt. As the locals who live on this beautiful island attest, Maui truly is heaven on earth.

The only problem is that Maui is also a very expensive place to visit. The beauty, popularity, weather and remote location of the Hawaiian Islands can exact a heavy financial demand on the tourist wallet, especially if you are an urban worker like me. If you are familiar with these high costs, you are most likely asking yourself: "What is the executive director of a charity that serves inner-city families doing in Hawaii? How did he get the money to pull off such a trip? I only wish I could do that."

These are all good questions, and by all practical measures, our trip should have been impossibility. After all, we certainly did not have the financial resources to be there. The airfare alone for a family of four costs a fortune from Toronto to Maui. Then add the costs of accommodations, food and a rental car—that is a lot of money I did not have. So, what were we doing in Hawaii and how did we get there? The answer is quite simple—God wanted us there and He made all the arrangements. I was in Hawaii because I needed to meet God—plain and simple. Little did I know how much this would come true.

Our trip to Hawaii was a gift. It was a week-long stopover on our way to Australia as part of our sabbatical we so desperately needed. We had flown out of Toronto on November 23 and were not to return until January 28. In other words, this was the trip of a lifetime—two months in Australia with a brief stopover in Hawaii. How could anyone top that? It was a dream come true. Needless to say, we were very excited to leave our city and enjoy a long time away as a family. What made this trip even more exciting was that, deep in our hearts, we knew that God wanted us to go. He even provided free airline tickets for us through a wonderful man who operated a successful business. This business person had lots of air mile points and offered them to fly us anywhere in the world. Australia was the perfect location for our sabbatical as I had wonderful friends there who offered places to stay, vehicles to use and, best of all, it was as far away from Toronto as possible.

As for Hawaii? Well, Hawaii was the ideal place to start our sabbatical, as these beautiful islands act as a stopover for jets to refuel on their way to Australia. What made Maui so enticing was the fact that we had another friend who, through his contacts, was able to get us a place to stay for free at the famous Hana-Maui Resort. This incredible and secluded oasis in Hana was very private, luxurious and extremely restful. A hidden gem well acquainted with the rich and famous who come to escape their demanding schedules for much needed R and R. Everything was provided for us and it would not cost us, or our ministry, one cent. What a wonderful gift from God. I am certain that God wanted us in Hawaii. After all, He provided the means for us to enjoy our sabbatical. He had made all the arrangements.

Now it is important to realize that I am not a sabbatical type of guy. Slowing down is not my style. I am a high-energy, type A, driven personality. When things get busy, I get energized. When things are chaotic, I am at my best. When time pressures are about to explode and there is complete havoc all around me, I am in my element. That is why I love urban ministry—nothing happens according to schedule. If you are a control freak, then urban ministry will drive you nuts. There is never enough money and not enough staff to deal with the myriads of ministry needs that pop up in the city.

Hurting people tend to find themselves constantly in trouble and trials never come according to some neat, controllable schedule. All it takes is one phone call and you are off to the races—another mother frantic because Children's Aid has come unexpectedly to take her child away. A young man you know has just been arrested and you need to be at court right away. A recent immigrant, who attends one of your programs, has an important government hearing available for review, right now, and you need to be there to vouch for her. A slimy landlord has threatened to kick one of the families you serve out of his building because the single mother had not conceded to his sexual advances and you must advocate for her immediately. The list of needs and awful circumstances in which people find themselves goes on and on. All these emergencies pop up unexpectedly, and you have to find a way to squeeze them into your busy schedule. The demands are great, time is limited and we urban workers feel that we must respond to these needs happening all around us as quickly as possible! That is just the way of urban ministry.

I never had any time to take or even think about a sabbatical. Who could take that much time off when you are far too busy saving the world? I was engaged in doing very important things and could not waste any of my valuable time to reflect on my life. To me, sabbaticals were for sissies. I was too strong for that and certainly had no need for it. Besides, there was no time to take a break in my hectic schedule for a sabbatical. Money had to be raised to keep UrbanPromise afloat. More community workers had to be recruited to meet our growing demands. Current staff needed encouragement, training and supervision. I had an extensive speaking schedule involving churches and youth conferences that invited me to challenge them to reach out to their own cities and communities. Finally, there were also the day-to-day operational responsibilities that had to be taken care of and the daily fires that had to be put out.

There is never any rest in urban missionary work. There are always constant ministry needs screaming for your attention. That was my life for years. Running, always running, to do things so that we as a ministry could be successful. The words of Jesus, "Come to me, all you who are weary and burdened, and I will give you rest" (Matthew 11:28, NIV), were a nice afterthought, but I was too busy to even come to Jesus for rest. I had important work to do. Perhaps one day, but up to this point in my life I felt I didn't need it and certainly had no time for it. This was the story of my life for years. Then, without my consent, my life came crashing down like a house of cards in a hurricane. It had been the busiest year of my life.

These two heart-wrenching tragedies, accompanied by the continual grind of ministry, had finally worn me out. I was ministering to everybody affected by these terrible losses and I felt that I was taking the hits for everyone while, at the same time, trying to deal with my own grief. Needless to say, I was in trouble. No one can prepare you for these types of tragedies. There are no easy answers, no quick fixes. All you are left with is the nagging question, "How do I get through this?"

What do you do when faced with these types of devastating realities, one after another? I'll tell you what I did. I went into overdrive. I just revved up my engine and did what I normally do when there is lots of work to be done. I immediately served like a madman, trying to be superhuman for everyone. The problem was that I was superhuman with the emphasis on *human*. For the first time in my life, I felt that all my activity and all my work was in vain. I wanted to run away from everything and everyone associated with these problems, but where do you run too? The effects on my personal life were frightening. I was now a broken and bleeding man, marred with too many scars of ministry to continue.

Finally, I had had enough. It was over. There was not one ounce of energy left. I was out of gas and I knew it. That in itself was surprising, as I usually don't have a clue when enough is enough and my poor family had paid the price in the past with a burned-out father and husband. However, this was different. The toll from these two tragedies was immense, and my family felt it too. My children were having nightmares. They knew what was happening. My poor wife was like a single mother for far too long as I was rarely home, as I was busy trying to keep up with all of the ministry demands surrounding me. The strong, independent super-pastor whom I thought I was had now become that despised sissy I had envisioned—a weakling in need of a sabbatical. However, this is *exactly* what I needed to become—a weakling—and that is exactly what God wanted me to be—feeble, humbled and broken before Him.

It was in this state of emotional brokenness that my family and I were in Hawaii, on a one-week stopover, on our way to a fabulous two-month family sabbatical in Australia. I was weary and heavily burdened and was finally coming to Jesus to get His rest that He promised.

So here I was, on the second day of the sabbatical, beaten, bruised and barely breathing. There was hardly a pulse left in my soul. Though I was feeling an immense darkness inside of me, outside it was a stunning morning. The tropical birds were out in full plumage, fluttering to and fro, singing to one another the joys of a new morning. It was then, while my children were still in their beds sleeping, that Judith and I finally had the chance to spend a few stolen minutes alone to talk. She motioned for me to join her out on the deck of our gorgeous beach house we had at the Hana – Maui Resort.

As we sat in our deck chairs, with the cool Pacific breeze blowing through the palm trees, my wife asked me an important question, the answer of which would later prove to be prophetic. Looking me in the eyes, she asked, "Colin, what do you want to get out of this sabbatical?" Without a thought, I impulsively replied, "Jude, I am 40 years old and I don't even know who I am."

I could tell that my response puzzled her. This is because my wife, like the majority of women, is more in touch with her soul than most men seem to be. Women, by nature, appear to be far more mature than men when it comes to self-awareness. This is where we get the expression *women's intuition*. Women naturally have that sixth sense to pick up on the character of others far more effectively than men simply because they are able to go deeper when it comes to concerns of the soul. And when it came to matters of the heart, my wife far exceeds me in every way. For her to be in the presence of a 40-year-old man who, by all outward appearances seemed to be a success, just admitted that he was not in touch with his own soul was a very sad and confusing admission for my wife to hear. Unlike me, she instinctively knew that success could never be measured by outward achievements. It could only be found in the interior life. Now here she was, talking to her husband who had been completely devastated by the trials of the previous months. His exterior successes were savagely ripped to shreds, and he had no interior foundation on which to rest his self-esteem and purpose. I was a clear example of a man who built his life on the sands of exterior appearances.

"But if you just use my words in Bible studies and don't work them into your life, you are like a stupid carpenter who built his house on the sandy beach. When a storm rolled in and the waves came up, it collapsed like a house of cards." (Matthew 7:26,27, The Message)

The winds of trials and tribulation of the previous months had blown my entire external life to pieces and there was nothing left on which to cling. My life was out of control. Trusting in exterior dependence left me vulnerable to the control of outward conditions and approval. But now the victories of my hard work amounted to nothing. I had lived my life for the cheers of those around me and not in step with the God who dwells in my soul. When these cheers ceased, so did my life. I was a shallow shell and no longer knew who I was. Though my wife wanted to immediately jump to Matters of the Soul 101, she wisely restrained herself and then, with great empathy and concern, asked, "How will you be able to know who you are?" My reply was even quicker this time. "I don't have a clue. God will have to take me there."

---◆---

"Two babies were born on the same day at the same hospital. They lay there and looked at each other. Their families came and took them away. Eighty years later, by a bizarre coincidence, they lay in the same hospital, on their deathbeds, next to each other. One of them looked at the other and said, 'So, what did you think?'"

– Steven Wright

A DAY AT THE BEACH

◆

CHAPTER ELEVEN

As a teenager, I used to play a strange game that my friends and I grimly called "the game of death." It was a silly adolescent conversational game that we would play at the local greasy spoon or in the basement of a friend's home. Out of strange curiosity, we would have long talks discussing how we preferred to experience our own death. The question: "What type of death would you want to experience?" was asked and then we would share our thoughts. My macho friends spoke of dying with great gusto through some gory experience like a plane crash or train wreck. When we listened to these guys, we knew that they were not being serious and that it was just a typical case of testosterone-driven bravado used to hide their fear of death. Those who were jokers wanted to be dressed up as clowns and placed in their caskets so that when visitation came, we would all have a great laugh. Most of us, the truly honest ones, wanted to die in our sleep at a very old age. I know that this was my dream death. That would be the best way to go for me. No pain. No suffering. Have a cup of tea and biscuits, then wobble into my bed with my wife and fall asleep on earth, only to wake up in heaven.

Unfortunately, we don't have any choice when it comes to how and when we will die.

Tragic days can often start out so perfectly, but end so badly. On my fateful day, the sun was shining, the birds singing and there was the immense beauty of Maui to enjoy. The temperature was a very comfortable 80 degrees Fahrenheit with a faint wind blowing the fragrance of the flowers growing everywhere on the island gently onto the exquisite beach. Perfect!

Our hotel was located in the old Hawaiian village of Hana, right on the coast of the Pacific Ocean. The surroundings of the resort were stunning with so many naturally beautiful things to see in the area. On the top of our "To See" list was Hamoa Beach—ranked as one of the most gorgeous beaches in the world. So on that fateful sunny morning we packed our car full of beach supplies and drove the short 10-minute drive to Hamoa, finding a spot to park on the coastal road that overlooked the beach.

As we made our way from our car through a small leafy pathway leading us downwards towards the ocean shore, we slowly saw the beach in all its glory. What a tremendous sight! Emerald–blue water cascading up and down to the rhythm of the waves that crashed onto the salt and pepper volcanic sand that made up the beach front. It was dazzling. I was so excited to spend the day at this postcard-beautiful, sun-drenched oasis.

When we got to the beach front, I couldn't help but notice the large waves that were powerfully crashing to the shoreline in majestic order, and I immediately thought how much fun it would be boogie boarding with the kids. For those of you who do not know what a boogie board is, let me describe it for you. A boogie board is a shorter and seemingly tamer version of a surfboard that you hold onto and lie on top of after catching a wave. You then surf head first into shore, riding the wave while lying on your stomach on top of the board.

I excitedly went to the cabana where they had the boogie boards available to be signed out by hotel guests. I talked to the man in charge and asked him in typical parent-like fashion if the water was safe and if the conditions were okay for boogie boarding. He replied that it was a perfect day for the beach and that the water conditions were completely safe. I was so excited. I had left cold wintry Canada for the sunshine, waves and wonder of Hawaii. To me, this ocean and its waves were what Hawaii was all about. I could not wait to enjoy a few great days at this beach with my family.

I quickly signed out three boards, one for my 10-year-old son C.J., the other for my 6-year-old daughter Victoria and the third for me. The attendant helped bring the boards to the beach and got us a spot with umbrellas to shade us from the sun. He got lounge chairs and dusted the sand off with a little beach broom as my wife and I chatted happily about the day ahead and the beauty of the beach.

The pressures of the city and our ministry were thousands of miles away, and I could feel the stress and turmoil of the past year slip off me like the beads of sweat that were beginning to slowly slide down the sides of my face. We were in Hawaii, and life couldn't have been any better than it was on that warm and sunny day. Finally, our chance to rewind after so many tension-filled months. We put on our sunscreen and finalized the setup for our beach day. The cooler was full of ice, cold drinks and fruit. Beside my lounge chair was a bag of potato chips, plenty of sand toys and books to read. Everything was wonderful—sun, family, snacks and the ocean. Finally, I could begin my sabbatical and rest, but before I would actually lie down with a book in hand, I wanted to first experience the warm waters of the Pacific.

I was ready for the ocean. It was beckoning me to come and play in its beautiful waters. I was excited, but before I went into the Hawaiian waters, for the first time in my life, I instinctively marked the moment by checking my watch. I wanted to remember the exact time I enjoyed the Hawaiian surf. I also was on a time constraint as I had promised my daughter Victoria that we would head back to the hotel later in the day for a lei-making class.

That class started at 1:00 p.m. and my watch read 11:20 a.m. Great. I had more than an hour to enjoy the ocean before I went with her to her class. I looked out at the beach and saw my children waiting for me while holding their boards and splashing about at the shoreline. Gripping my board, I ran to the ocean like a professional surfer and told my kids to watch Daddy first before they tried theirs. Looking back, I can't help but laugh at those words: "Watch Daddy first before you try this." Who did I think I was? A pro? They watched Daddy alright, and now I doubt they would ever try this thing again.

I was so energized because the waves were huge. My thinking was based on total ignorance. I, a city slicker from the Great White North of Canada, actually believed that the bigger the wave, the better the ride. I really thought that these big waves would be kind enough to give me a fun little ride, politely pushing me to shore with their benevolent power. Boy, was I wrong. As I ran towards the pounding surf and past my son C.J. I heard him tell me that he didn't think it was a good idea to go in the water. It was as if he had a premonition. Here was a 10-year-old boy warning his 40-year-old father, who should be wisened by the years of life experience, to be careful. My son, in his typical sensitivity, was worried about our safety. He is an incredibly responsible kid with the insights to see the possible negative effects of the what-ifs of life from every angle. Unfortunately, I didn't listen to his wise words of warning and threw off his concerns as another typical, unwarranted, childish fear.

I went right into the surf and watched the swimmers ahead of me having fun surfing, boogie boarding and body surfing. I noticed they were much further out than I was. I now realize why. They were seasoned locals and knew that if they caught a big wave and got dumped by its mighty power, they would be safe because they would have more water in which to land and cushion their fall. They had what I lacked—wisdom of experience. All I had was an adventurous spirit and no experience regarding Hawaiian ocean water safety. This was a terrible and dangerous mix.

I went into the water at about chest depth and looked for a wave to catch. They were huge, nothing like what I was used to while vacationing off the Florida or Carolina coastlines. I loved boogie boarding on my previous vacations to the Atlantic Ocean, but these Pacific waves were bigger, stronger and came up much more frequently, To me that meant more fun, more of a ride. I thought that I could boogie board just like I did when I vacationed at the Atlantic.

The first wave knocked me down and I wrenched my knee. It was twisted and painful, but I bravely shook it off. I thought to myself that a little wonky knee would never stop me. I was in Hawaii for the first and most likely last time of my life, and so I was committed to enjoying the beach, even in pain. That injury alone should have been a warning, but I have never been the type to be slowed down by a little pain.

Though it now registered in my brain that these waves were definitely different than any waves I had ever experienced, I continued onwards. I limped to Judith, wincing and laughing while telling her what had just happened to my knee, and then quickly returned to the water more determined then ever to catch the "big one." Waiting to time the perfect wave, I let a few blow past me by diving under them.

My timing was off. All of a sudden, I saw it from a distance, churning towards me at great speed and growing larger as it got closer. I jumped on and knew immediately that I was in trouble. I thought that I had caught it while it had peaked, but it kept going higher and higher. It was about twice my height and was getting taller. I felt like a speck of dust on top of it.

With me on top, it grew larger, and as it grew, it got closer and closer to the shoreline. I knew that this meant it would eventually have to break into shallow water. I would be dumped towards the ocean floor without the benefit of deeper water to cushion my fall. But I had no control or ability to get off this momentous wave. As if reading my mind, the wave suddenly curled into a C formation and threw me down like a jackhammer slicing apart the water with brute force, driving my head into the sand. I felt it snap as it hit the hard sandy bottom. Immediately, my body churned in the surf, twisting and turning like a sock in the spin cycle. Suddenly, I was surrounded by bubbles and clouds of sand that danced together in a watery waltz to the music of the ringing in my ears.

I could feel no pain. My body was numb as I floated beneath the water's surface. Then, as my body stopped tumbling about, to and fro, from the mighty force of the wave, I realized that I was slowly floating downwards. It was then that my ringing ears played a new song. I heard a droning, foghorn-like noise as the water around me calmed down from the passing of the crashing wave. My immediate reaction was to swim to the surface, but I couldn't move a muscle. I was paralyzed.

I have read of people's near-death experiences where, within seconds, the history of their lives flashed before their eyes and they saw a bright light at the end of a dark tunnel. I did not have this experience. My near-death experience seemed to make everything slow down. Once my body stopped churning around, I slowly floated to the bottom of the ocean, and time stood still. It was surreal—as if everything were in slow motion. I felt I was outside of my body, a painless observer to what was happening below. In this state of paralysis, I experienced what I can only describe as an out-of-body experience where I saw my body face down in the sand of the ocean floor. It was like my spirit was knocked right out of my body, detached by the force of the impact when the wave slammed me into the ground. I was floating, motionless, the droning, ringing sound in my ears, the sight of bubbles all around me, and the taste of froth from the sea inside my mouth. I was drowning and could do nothing about it.

My brain was screaming at my body to swim! Move! Get out of the water as fast as possible! But my body refused to listen. I was in deep trouble. My body lay there, face down on the bottom of the seabed, unable to move. My brain was on high alert, yelling commands at my body to get moving, swim, get to the surface where there was oxygen to breathe and my family to see again. However, my body was not responding to my brain's orders. It was like it was on strike refusing to go back to work. One thing I will never forget is watching my arms. While telling them to move, they just floated from the front of my body to the sides, totally limp. My brain was working fine, doing what it was supposed to do, instructing my body to swim to safety. However, my arms and legs were not listening. I was at the mercy of the elements of the sea.

People often ask me what it was like to be drowning. I tell them that I always thought drowning would be a terrible way to die. It was certainly not one of the options when I played the death game of my adolescence. However, now that I was actually experiencing it, I have to admit it was very peaceful. In fact, when I first hit my head and realized I was paralyzed, I got angry with myself. *Great! Now you did it. You just ruined this trip for everybody.*

Looking back, I can't believe my first thoughts were to worry about the trip for my family. However, even though I was at death's door, I felt great. I had an unexplainable peace. Then I prayed: *God, I am going to see You soon unless by some miracle You get me out of here.*

There was no desperation in my prayer. No urgency or desire to be rescued. I was experiencing a state of calm and peace that I have never before experienced in my life. I felt great. I was ready to die and meet my God and all was well. While I was drowning, I thought, *So this is what death feels like?* It was a strange sensation. I also felt another presence with me under those warm ocean waters. It was if there were a spiritual presence of goodness and darkness with me, and I often wonder if there were angels under those waves. I felt like an observer of another realm, watching an angel of life and an angel of death facing off over my destiny. It was as if they were staring at each other curiously, not knowing what the next step would be. I felt confused, wondering if death were about to take me away. Death seemed just as baffled as I was. These spiritual warriors, life and death, seemed to be eyeing each other up and down like two boxers feeling their opponent out during the first minutes of a title fight. Feinting punches, nervously bobbing back and forth, to and fro, but neither one throwing the first punch.

When was death going to make its move? What was it waiting for? What power do I have to fight back? Though in my mind I wanted to live, it was peaceful, tranquil, heavenly. No fear, no struggle, no worries. I was okay. It was then that I thought of our little camper who had drowned just a few months before. I was now going through the same experience he did. At that point, I started thinking of what would happen to me. I was in a state of tranquility while also thinking of the various possibilities open to me for my survival. Most of these possibilities were grim long shots. One question I had concerned the waves that were crashing above my limp body. I wondered if they would push me slowly to shore or draw me back out to the ocean depths. I also wondered how long it would take before anyone noticed my situation. I doubted whether anyone, other than my son, saw me get pummelled by the wave. I could not remember anyone near me when I was in the surf that could have possibly seen my accident. The only people I saw in the water were way ahead of me in the deeper regions and not within eyesight of a drowning man, unable to move, motion for help or even yell. A submerged, paralyzed body, hidden by rough-strewn seas would be hard to see, especially on a secluded beach. What made matters worse was that all the swimmers were far ahead of me in deeper surf, laughing with each other and certainly not looking to shore, but out to sea. The odds were very slim for me to get out of the water alive.

Though I had this amazing peace, I still wanted to live. I saw the ocean water swirling around me, and though my brain was telling my body to swim, I couldn't move a finger or toe. I heard a droning in my head, felt a numbness in my body, saw bubbles and felt myself slowly rise and then sink again to the bottom from the motion of the waves above me. I was drifting slowly downwards, blowing in a rhythm of back and forth motion, held alight by the water and the waves, slowly descending to the sandy bottom. I was like a leaf in autumn at the mercy of nature, unable to choose where to land. And like that leaf left rotting on the forest floor, I was alone, left to die on the sand under the waves of Hamoa Beach.

All of a sudden, I noticed that I was in shallow waters. My forehead was pushed into the sand, and my chin was driven into my chest. From this position I was able to see my torso resting on sand. *Was it a wave that somehow picked me up from under the water and brought me to the shore? Perhaps it was an angel pushing me upwards towards the safety of the sandy edge of the beach?* I didn't know how I got to this shallow water line. All I knew was that my chances of being rescued had now greatly improved. The only problem was that I was face down, drowning in shallow water. While in this state, I thought that all I had to do was rock my body so that it could turn over and I would be on my back, able to breathe again. But again, my body refused to listen to my brain. All I could do was just lie there, my face buried in the sand in water no deeper than a foot! Then the strangest thing happened. When I could no longer hold my breath for one more second, I was flipped over onto my back.

My 220-pound body easily turned over and I saw sunshine and gulped air back into my deflated lungs. I was able to get one desperate and well-timed gasp of salty and watery air. *Could this be the first punch, the first move? Did I catch death by surprise? Did the angels throw a glancing blow? Did death blink first?*

It was then that I saw C.J.'s face. The wave rested my limp body about 15 feet in front of him. He was staring, open mouthed, right at me. In his shock, he was more paralyzed at the sight of me then I ever was. I can only imagine, from reading the look on his face, that this little boy was in the throes of extreme trauma. A 10-year-old athletic boy, who loved to be active and play lots of sports with his father, tends to think his dad is a superman, a man of steel, unable to be injured. Death is not a component of life on which 10-year-olds have a grip. To young boys, fathers are idolized and are little gods who can always work out problems. This is what 10-year-old boys see when they are with their father—divine control, safety and security. Now all of his ideals were in shambles because of one wave. Superman had now faced his kryptonite. He was dying, and this boy's now ripped-apart world of security had left him as paralyzed as his superman father.

C.J.'s reaction was my wakeup call. What I saw on his face I will never forget. It was awful a frozen look of fear and hopelessness. Seeing his face and that look of shock at his father drowning was unbearable for me. That look on his face has been burned into my soul forever and I will never forget it. I was now in dread—not for myself, but for *his* sake, my daughter's sake, my wife's sake! I felt a surge of energy, driven by emotion welling up inside and I tried to scream for help as I gasped for air, but all that came out of my mouth was a strained whisper. Though my brain was now screaming at the top of its lungs, "Help, C.J. Help," I could only hear my words come out in a rasp, a scratch. My diaphragm was partially paralyzed from the trauma to my neck. Without this muscle, I could not push out the proper amount of air into my vocal chords to make them ring out loudly in a desperate cry for assistance. No one could hear me yell for help. Even worse, I was now having difficulty breathing. Then, after a few seconds, I was quickly washed back into deeper waters. The undertow had taken me back into the ocean depths. This was the cruellest of all blows. I had been within a few inches' reach of life, but was now back under the water, unable to get out, drowning yet again. In a span of seconds, my sabbatical was over and I was once again fighting for my life under a watery grave. How could this be happening to me? A murder, a drowning and now this. I was about to lose my life, my wife, my children and my future.

———————————— ◆ ————————————

"'Dude, like I went over the falls and totally pearled....' Much as surfers have their own peculiar lingo, they also incur an array of injuries from the sport that can be just as peculiar to physicians."

– Radiological Society of North America,
Dec. 1, 2004 at www.sciencedaily.com

GOING OVER THE FALLS

◆

CHAPTER TWELVE

Hawaii is the jewel of the Pacific. A stretch of approximately eight main islands that bask in the sun like precious stones. These breathtaking islands burst forth from the ocean, full of stunning rain forests, waterfalls, flowers and beaches. They are surrounded by incredible emerald-blue water and are actually the tips of huge, underwater mountains that jut out of the ocean. They are the most remote islands in the world. No other body of land is as isolated. They are separated by the longest stretch of ocean than any other land mass and are therefore on the receiving end of the most powerful waves in the world. This great expanse of water allows time and distance to form and empower waves to build up momentum before crashing on the shores of Hawaii's beaches. This natural phenomena means that the waves of Hawaii are unique only to Hawaii. In other words, there are no waves like them anywhere else, and it is for this reason that people come from all over to surf these magnificent waves.

"Going over the falls" is surfing lingo used to describe someone who catches a large wave at the wrong time, causing their body to be propelled straight down into the ground with great force.

According to David North, Staff, Medical Physics of Rhode Island Hospital, going over the falls is a very dangerous experience:

"There is a critical moment when you should **not** catch a wave. Generally this is when a wave has formed into a C and is throwing water forwards at high speed. If you catch the wave at this point, you'll be treated to a new experience: Going Over the Falls."[1]

123

This is exactly what happened to me. You can just picture it—me on top of a huge waterfall being thrown over its edge, onto the rocky escarpment below. I only wish I read this advice before I destroyed my body. I did everything he warns not to do. I caught the wave, in textbook "how not to" fashion. I actually threw myself on top of it while it was growing larger and larger, higher and higher, into its dreaded C. Then I went right over the falls into the ocean floor with a horrendous thud. Instead of the wave pushing me forwards for a wonderful ride, it actually drove me, head first, straight down to the ground. Believe me when I tell you that going over the falls is a violent pummelling of the human body. I know because it happened to me.

Going over the falls has no respect for the law of gravity. It is far more violent. I didn't just drop from the wave into the water. It actually picked me up and lifted my body up to its peak. Then it furiously slammed my body straight down into the ocean floor with great contempt. It was as if the wave had been personally offended that I had enough gall to think that I could actually take advantage of its power and go for a nice little ride.

I researched the type of force involved when a wave picks a human body up and, at its peak, slams it downwards into the sea. To understand how much power is generated by a wave, we need to understand how waves are formed. According to Robert H. Stewart at the Department of Oceanography, Texas A&M University:

> "How high the wave finally becomes will depend on three things: the wind velocity or speed, how long a time the wind blows, and the total distance over which the wind can blow on the water, called the 'fetch.' So, large waves are made by strong winds acting over long distances. Generally, the biggest waves are made by large storms that are well out at sea. In general, normal waves (not storm driven) are bigger in the Pacific because the Pacific is bigger and the winds have more fetch. That is the reason why the best waves for surfing are usually on the coasts of Hawaii, which is a group of islands out in the middle of the Pacific."[2]

Just my luck! I just so happened to be visiting the best place in the world to go over the falls. I was where the strongest and most dangerous waves in the entire world make their presence known. The further the wave travels, the more force it can build up and the more power it can unleash. Since Hawaii is thousands and thousands of miles from the nearest land mass, its waves have plenty of time to form way out in the Pacific before they crash, unobstructed, onto the Hawaiian coastline.

But how much horsepower is generated by a wave? According to POEMS:

"Put simply, a wave is a traveling disturbance. Ocean waves travel for thousands of kilometres through the water. Kinetic energy, the energy of motion, in waves is tremendous. An average 4-foot, 10-second wave striking a coast puts out more than 35,000 horsepower per mile of coast."[3]

That is a lot of horsepower. The wave that drilled my head into the sand was much higher than four feet. That would be, according to the scientific calculations in the above quotation, well over 35,000 horsepower involved in sledgehammering my head into the ocean floor! When you put my accident in those terms, all I can say is—Ouch! And that I must have a very hard head.

The good news is that most people who are injured in this way survive. They come out of the experience with a mouthful of salty water—no worse for wear—just a little dizzy. They float back to the surface scared, exhausted, but laughing at the experience. They were probably in deep enough water and, therefore, didn't get thrown straight down into the ocean floor where serious injuries can occur.

Others are not as fortunate. They get slammed by the wave and actually hit the hard bottom of the ocean floor. When they come to the surface, they are groggy, have a sore head or a sand-scraped face or possibly a bruised or dislocated shoulder. Then they find their surfboard floating nearby and go back out into the surf after saying to their surfing buddies, "Dude, I went over the falls!"

And then there are people like me who fare a lot worse. Because they were in shallow waters, the law of physics of the movable object hitting the unmovable land mass comes into effect. When this happens with that type of force, terrible results happen—unconsciousness, broken necks, paralysis, drowning and death. I call this a level three falls experience. Level one is a rush. Level two a trip. Level three is a tragedy. I had a level three falls experience.

---

[1] Taken from article by David North, Staff, Medical Physics, Rhode Island Hospital.

[2] Taken from an article from the Department of Oceanography, Texas A&M University, Robert H. Stewart, stewart@ocean.tamu.edu, All contents copyright© 1996, 1998, 2002 Robert H. Stewart, All rights reserved.

[3] Taken from article by the Practical Ocean Energy Management Systems, Inc., (POEMS) a California 501I(3) nonprofit philanthropic stewardship organized to educate the general public on the importance of developing ocean energy.

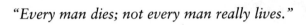

"Every man dies; not every man really lives."

– William Wallace

THE RESCUE

◆

CHAPTER THIRTEEN

The water crashed over me and sucked me back under the surf. I had been so close to the refuge of dry land only to be pulled back out by the power of the tide. I began to sink again, and with each second came terror. The peace I had initially felt when drowning in the deeper waters was now replaced by fear. This time I was panic-stricken. My son's frozen figure on the beach had been a wakeup call for me and revealed to me an important reason to live. I was no longer at peace with dying, but it was too late. There was nothing I could do about it. I couldn't choose life. I was paralyzed, unable to move, and I was sinking once again deep into a watery grave. I had experienced drowning and then encountered life again by being washed up on the shore. For an instant, I was able to catch a breath and see my son. Hope was again restored. Then, all of a sudden, I was thrown back into the water, only to drown again. It was the cruellest of ironies. What made this even worse was that my last dying thought was the picture of my son's horror-stricken face, staring back at me in shock. This was a horrible way to die. Once again, the water surrounded my body and I sank down, deeper and deeper, but this time my descent was quicker as I had less air in my lungs to help me float. The paralysis of my diaphragm had taken its toll. I was finished. Just as I was about to give up all hope, I saw a bright light flashing through the water like a flashlight shining in a foggy night. Was this the light at the end of the tunnel that people describe they experienced when talking about their near-death experiences?

All of a sudden, wonderful, miraculous hands grabbed my limp shoulders and quickly lifted my body up through the watery depths. The light got brighter and brighter until, with a sudden burst, my face felt warm, beautiful, life-giving air. I saw a bright blue sky that never looked so good. My rescue had begun.

I never saw the face of the person who was first on the scene of my rescue. What I did see was his hands, his beautiful, providential, life-saving hands that had first brought life to my oxygen depleted body. To this day, I still haven't met him. This is because in the middle of his rescue effort, another stranger appeared. I remember hearing the voice of this second rescuer yelling at the top of his lungs that he was a doctor. He quickly took over the delicate task of getting my limp body out of the waves.

Nearly every day I think of this man who initially saved my life. I wish I could thank him personally and shake the hands that had pulled me so gently from my watery crypt. Witnesses tell me that he was a local, but as soon as the doctor took over, he humbly disappeared and I was never able to thank him for his wonderful act of kindness. One day, I hope to meet this modest hero and if I do, I know I will cry many, many tears of gratitude.

In the midst of a growing crowd of curious onlookers, I was slowly taken out of harm's way. I heard the strong and reassuring voice of the doctor who had taken over my rescue. He told everyone that his name was Eric while he boldly took charge of things by barking out his medical credentials to everyone. I was extremely comforted when I heard him tell the increasing throng that he was an emergency room doctor on vacation from California and that his specialty was surf injuries.

Eric was good at his job. He knew what he was doing. His skills were clearly evident in how he took control of the situation while supporting my neck from further damage. I found it very comforting to be in his care as I saw how everyone listened to his authoritative words. He was a true leader, demanding of respect. From his actions and the tone of his voice, I knew that God had placed him here, at this beach, at that time. God certainly does provide! This doctor knew what he was doing and he did it well. Eric's confidence and calm professionalism were a tremendous source of calm for me. He was on top of things and knew exactly how to treat victims of spinal-cord injuries.

While caring for me and trying to coach the rest of the people to be more of a help than a hindrance, he firmly declared that they needed to listen to him as things didn't look very good for me. If you were there that day, you would have thought that this was bad news. However, to me these words rang with hope.

With all of this pandemonium, I could barely hear C.J. weeping. He was extremely upset and crying near my pale, bloated body, screaming and sobbing: "I don't want my Daddy to die! I don't want my Daddy to die! I want to go back to Toronto! I just want to go home!"

Buried in the crowd of shocked and worried faces staring down at me, I could also sense my little daughter Victoria standing nearby. I couldn't turn my head to see her because of the extent of my neck injury, but I just knew she was near. Later, while at the hospital, Judith told me that my little girl was stunned, quiet and very stoic throughout the entire rescue. One person I did see clearly was Judith. She was able to cut through the crowd and regularly stretch herself over me so that her eyes were inches from my face. She would then repeatedly tell me, with tears in those eyes, how much she loved me and that I was going to be alright. My wife was frantically doing all she could to help the children and, at the same time, comfort me. I remember her waving her hand over my face and praying to God to heal me.

Throughout this nightmare, through the buzzing crowd and ongoing confusion, I felt her love and prayers. My wife is truly the greatest blessing of my life and she kept me calm and provided me with the hope I so desperately needed. It was amazing to see and hear how she automatically went right into crisis mode, a state of being with which we youth workers have much experience, in which we are able to control ourselves in the midst of very intimidating circumstances. Through blurred and teary eyes, I kept seeing her pop back and forth from comforting my children to encouraging me to keep living. This took incredible inner strength and she proved it on that sunny day.

Later, she told me about a woman who was standing beside her while she was scurrying back and forth. This complete stranger took on the role of an angel and was there for my wife throughout this ordeal, talking to her and comforting her, telling her that she would stay with her and help in any way she could. Those types of words comfort a dying man, as he knows there are people there to protect and provide for his family when he is unable to be there for them.

Concerned faces of all ages were staring down at me. Voices were excitedly speaking back and forth in a cacophony of confusion. In the midst of this spinning mob of people, I was able to see and hear Eric asking me how my breathing was and if I could move my fingers and toes. I could barely speak loud enough to answer his questions as my voice trailed off in a slurring whisper. My breathing was getting worse. I tried to wiggle a finger, then a toe, but nothing. In the back of my mind, a horrible thought was beginning to take form. I began to realize that I was dying right here on the beach from suffocation. My diaphragm was tingling and with it my breathing became more laboured as I wheezed little breaths, each one weaker than the one before. How ironic I thought my death was going to be. Rescued from a watery tomb only to die from suffocation right here, in front of a crowd of strangers with my wife and children watching me slowly die. It was truly a horrific place in which to be.

As I was thinking of this, Eric would interrupt my thoughts by telling me his ongoing prognosis while assisting me. It was as if I were in an emergency room back in his hospital in California. He barked out his diagnosis to everyone within earshot of my wilted body stating that it appeared to him that I had heavy damage to my C3-C7 vertebrae of the spinal column in my neck. This diagnosis was quite scary as it meant that my paralysis also involved my diaphragm, since this part of the neck sends out impulses to the diaphragm muscle instrumental in breathing. As I lay on the beach, I felt my stomach tingling as my breathing became more and more of a struggle. I remembered that this was exactly what had happened to Christopher Reeve, the famous actor who starred in the "Superman" series of movies in the 1980s. He had a similar injury, the result of landing on his head after falling off a horse while show riding. He became a quadriplegic and needed to have a ventilator inserted into his throat to allow him to breathe. Once again, I began to believe that this was the end. I knew that if the paralysis continued to extend deeper in this region of my body, I would soon suffocate. Though my mind was telling my diaphragm muscles to move, to open up my lungs to be filled with life-giving air, they were having a difficult time responding. My breathing was getting worse. I quickly thought to myself that soon I would never see my family again and the final memory they would have of me was watching their husband and father gasping for air, slowly fading away before their very eyes.

Finally, a group of paramedics arrived on the scene with a spinal board and I was slowly dragged on top. They then taped my head from the top of my forehead to the hard wooden board and carried my lifeless form from the beach, up the hill, and placed me into a waiting ambulance. It had an oxygen kit set up, just waiting for me in the back of the vehicle. The paramedics quickly put it to good use by placing the mask over my mouth to help me to breathe. While all this was happening, Judith was asked if she would like to join me in the ambulance. The only catch was that there was only enough room for her. The children would have to stay behind with someone to care for them.

My wife valiantly chose to stay with her children, telling the paramedics, "The kids need me more right now. My husband is in God's hands." Then the sirens wailed, and I was quickly whisked off to the small medical clinic in the nearest town. I remember the white vinyl of the ambulance ceiling as all I could do was look straight up, since my head was taped solid to the spinal board. I also remember how my body shook to and fro, up and down, along the rough, bumpy and winding road from Hamoa. Twenty minutes later, I arrived at the small medical clinic in Hana. This was a little office building that did not have the equipment to deal with my type of emergency. It looked like it could handle the common cold, but life-threatening paralysis was well out of its league.

The good news was that it was equipped with a helipad, and within minutes I heard the loud churning sound of blades cutting a swath through the air as a helicopter landed nearby. I was then slowly placed into its belly and was soon in the air. Once again, all I could do was look straight up at the ceiling and see the faces of the two medical personnel who had taken over from the original paramedics. They watched over me, compared notes and talked with each other. I strained to hear what they were saying, as I was curious to find out what was happening to me. At this point, I still didn't know if I was going to make it, as breathing was still very difficult for me to do on my own. However, I could not hear a thing, as the noise inside the heli-

copter was far too loud. Every now and then, one of them would lean close to my ear and yell, asking me how I was feel*ing*. *That's a strange question,* I thought. *How can a paralyzed person feel anything?*
I had time to think as I lay there. My thoughts leapt about inside my head. All I wanted was to stay alive. While in the helicopter, I noticed that my breathing was getting a little better thanks to the oxygen mask. At that point, I knew that I was going to live and was happy for that. I didn't really care that I was paralyzed. In fact, I truly believed that I would remain paralyzed for the rest of my life. I knew how hard I hit that ocean floor. I felt the initial pain of my head being driven straight back into my shoulders after the impact. I remembered the strange backwards flip of my contorted body under the water after my head bounced off the bottom, twisting my body in an awkward arch as I flipped out of control under the water.

My survivor instincts had kicked in, and I was looking at my situation in a much simpler light. First, I was just hoping to stay alive while gasping for breath. But now with the oxygen mask on and my breathing getting better, I was confident I was going to live and that was all that was important to me at that point. I remember thinking that life in a wheelchair was a bonus! At least I would be able to see my wife and kids again. I was just thankful to be alive.

Then I began to wonder about other things. *Did I have enough medical insurance to pay for all of this medical care?* I was calculating how much money the helicopter trip would cost. I was thinking about the expenses for the medical attention I was about to receive at the hospital, and how much it would cost to care for the ongoing medical issues that would come with being a quadriplegic. However I wasn't worried. I figured that if worse came to worse and our insurance coverage was poor, I could sell the house and we could start life all over again in a small apartment. At that point, money wasn't much of a concern. I was alive, I would see my wife and kids again, and that was what was important.

While I was in the helicopter, Judith and the children remained at Hamoa Beach, left alone in their grief. Medical expenses were far from their minds. I had just been whisked off in front of their eyes, and now my traumatized wife was left with two distressed little ones. Her husband and their father was now gone, and all they had was a terrible memory of his bloated, pale and rasping body, gasping for air. They were stunned, lost on a beach in the middle of Hawaii, with no clue what to do next. They did not know where the hospital was or even how to get there. The people on the beach slowly walked past my wife and children, who were huddled together, still in a state of shock.

My wife turned to the woman who was such a great comfort to her during the rescue and asked, "What do I do now?" This compassionate good Samaritan offered to drive my family to the hospital, but Judith realized that all our baggage was still at the hotel. She knew that we were not returning to the resort to continue our sabbatical. Our trip was over, and she would need to bring our belongings back with her to the hospital. It was then that an attendant from the hotel arrived at the beach and drove my family back to get our things. There, with the help of other hotel staff, they packed two months of clothing into our suit-cases. Then she and the kids got into our small rental car and, with a man from the hotel as her driver, left for the long two-hour drive to be with me. She was on her way to meet up with her future destiny—life with no husband, a severely incapacitated husband or, if by miracle, a healthy one. It didn't look too good from her perspective and she pre-pared for the worst. As they travelled along the long, winding road to the hospital, she couldn't help but ponder how to tell the children that their father was dead and how this corresponded with the truth that God is a good God. There was a real possibility that this was to be their future as a family. The other possibility, which she entertained in her mind, was how life would be with a quadriplegic spouse. By all appear-ances, only one of these two realities awaited them at the hospital.

The helicopter ride was about 20 minutes from Hana, on one side of Maui, to the other side of the island where the Maui Memorial Hospital is located in the town of Wailuku. We landed in a baseball sta-dium known as Maui Memorial Stadium, where more paramedics were waiting for me to swiftly take me to the hospital just down the road.

All I could see was the blinding light of the sun that quickly dis-solved into the bland yellowing colour of the ceiling in the hospital hall-ways. It is a strange experience being unable to feel anything from the neck down and only able to see life buzz by you from the perspective of an emergency ambulance cot. With my head still strongly taped to the spinal board, I was forced to look straight up and bob my eyes back and forth to see the commotion all around me. I was quickly rushed through the hospital, my body moving forwards and swaying up and down, to and fro, through a myriad of hallways and doors, while all the while being surrounded by concerned voices talking about me. In the midst of all this action, I was unable to lift a finger or speak through the oxygen mask strapped to my face. All I could do was look straight up at the panorama of images that appeared in my view. All the images of the past hour flashed through my mind. A huge wave, sand, water, bubbles, my son's face, more water, light, blue sky, concerned faces, my wife, Victoria, ambulance and helicopter ceilings, more blue skies and sunshine, then hospital ceilings, concerned faces of doctors and nurses, machines, wires, tubes, etc. All circling my face and all mixed in under a canopy of noise.

When I arrived at the ER, everything continued in a hurried haze of organized chaos. I was hurried down some barren hallways through two large swinging doors into a room where a team of doctors, nurses and x-ray technicians awaited me. They did a great job of snipping off my swim trunks, cleaning all the sand off of me with a little vacuum cleaner, all the while peppering me with questions, checking my breathing and blood pressure and poking around my body.

Soon I was whisked down another hallway for a battery of x-rays, MRIs and CAT scans. By now, I was beginning to feel a little tingling return to my feet and arms. That was good news. About an hour later, after the x-rays, I lay motionless on the stainless steel ER table, waiting to hear the results. Finally, a doctor came in and looked down at me with a very confused look on his face. He then told me, three times, that I was "one lucky duck." Those were his exact words: *Lucky duck.* He told me that he had seen the initial x-rays and it was apparent that I did not break my neck. To him I was lucky because I was not dead or left a quadriplegic. He told me that the neurological specialist would assess the damage and let me know the extent of my injuries and their future repercussions on my quality of life.

Though it looked like there would be some sustaining injuries and a long rehab ahead, I was in much better shape than anyone expected. But I knew two things. First, I wasn't a duck, and second, luck had nothing to do with it. I was blessed and I let the doctor know it! I told him that for some reason, unknown to me, my life had been spared. In reality, I should have been dead, but here I was—alive! Why? I do not know. All that I did know at the time was that I was in the Critical Care Unit of Maui Memorial Hospital, instead of enjoying the beauty of Hawaii. I came to Maui on a sabbatical designed to restore my soul after a very tough year of heart-wrenching ministry. However, fate had changed my plans and here I was, waiting to hear more details regarding the length of my recovery and what kind of lasting injuries I had sustained. My future diagnosis was to come and time would reveal how and if I would recover.

While the medical staff cared for me, my family finally arrived at the hospital after their two-hour journey. To my wife's horror, she was met in the Emergency waiting room by a police officer and two social workers who were waiting for them. Judith knew, from her vast experience in our ministry, that this type of welcoming party usually meant bad news and her heart sank. She knew why they were there. Hospitals have social workers and police officers on call to deal with death situations. One social worker was assigned to my wife while the other specialized in childhood trauma. They sat and talked together, waiting to hear the news of my condition. Time passed slowly—agonizingly slow.

Eventually, a doctor arrived and told them my initial diagnosis. Though my neck wasn't broken, things were still a little fuzzy at that point. There was still extensive harm done to my neck and lots of accompanying nerve damage. Only time would reveal how fast I would recover and how well I would be able to walk and use my hands again. The bottom line was that I was alive and in good spirits. He then told them that they could visit me. He brought them in and we had one great reunion. What a relief it was to see them again! When we first saw each other, we just wept. I was alive and I was with the most precious possessions I had—my family.

C.J. was sad and I asked him what was wrong. He replied that he didn't help me when I was in the water and that he just stood there and watched me drown. He was full of shame because he never took action to try to save me. How could you blame a 10-year-old child for what he did? He was more paralyzed than I was as he was in a state of shock, watching what had happened. I told him that he very well may have saved my life through his body language. I believe that I was not the only person that saw the look of shock on his face when I was first washed up onto the beach that day. When I was too paralyzed to cry out for help, his face cried out for me. To this day, I believe that the man who first rescued me saw the trauma broadcasted on his face and looked over to see what he was staring at. C.J.'s reaction to my drowning was a neon sign pointing to my floating body at Hamoa Beach. If it weren't for him, no one would have looked into the water to see me drowning. I told my son he was a hero and thanked him for saving my life. It was good to see a smile appear on his face when he heard those words of encouragement. Victoria was very curious about all of the wires, tubes and medical monitors that were going in and out of my body, and told me with great pride that she never cried any tears for me as she knew that whatever happened, God was watching over me. She was right.

During our visit, the neurological specialist arrived with more detailed news about what was going on inside my nervous system. He described, in layman's terms, that the blunt force to my head had caused substantial damage to my neck. Apparently, I had three bulging herniated disks located between the C3 and C7 vertebrae of my neck. Amazingly, this was the same diagnosis that Eric, the ER doctor from California, had given me when I lay motionless on the sands of Hamoa Beach! On top of the damage in my neck, I also had a spinal column that was completely swollen shut. The nerve signals from my brain were cut off at the neck, stopping them from getting to my arms, hands and legs. This is why I was paralyzed.

I also had some very serious nerve damage to contend with. The specialist told me that because of this, there was a good chance that I would never get back 100 percent use of my hands or legs. Time was of the essence as the inflammation in my neck had to first subside in order to distinguish the true extent of the neurological damage. As the swelling in my spinal column decreased, I would see an improvement in my motor skills since there would be more space available in my spinal column and discs. This would leave more room to allow my brain signals to reach my arms, hands, legs and feet. The true prognosis of my recovery would be seen in the days to come.

I was told that the quicker I had movement back in my body, the higher the chances were for me to be close to a full recovery. Later, while meeting with one of my neurologists back in Toronto, I was once again amazed at God's provision. It appeared from the x-rays that the wave pummelled me into the sand at a perfect 90-degree angle. It was as if I performed a perfect dive with incredible form. The x-rays revealed that my head was compressed into my body on impact and went into my shoulders in a down-and-up accordion-like motion. This is why I was alive. If my head had been planted in the sand at any other angle, no matter how slight, my neck would have snapped in half and I would have died. Simple as that.

This was only one of many amazing providential events that occurred during my accident. I believe that God, for some unknown reason, spared my life. Later, during my recovery, I wrote down a list of all the so-called *coincidences* that happened to me. It is clear that from the list below that there are far too many coincidences to make it a coincidence.

Ten Reasons Why I Should Have Died

1. My neck should have broken if it were not for the perfect angle at which I hit the ocean floor.

2. I should have been unconscious from the impact of the ocean floor. My head was ringing and I was dizzy, but I never blacked out. If I had, I would have swallowed water and never surfaced.

3. I didn't panic and swallow water.

4. My diaphragm never became fully paralyzed, and so I was able to breathe, if only barely.

5. There was no strong undertow. I was not sucked deeper into the water.

6. I had a secondary wave push me to the shore when I surfaced.

7. When drowning in the shallow water, I had a secondary wave flip me over onto my back so I could take in more air. This occurred just as I lost my breath.

8. The accident took place on the Thanksgiving weekend. This usually abandoned beach had more people there than usual on that day.

9. I was told that the emergency helicopter medivac was just put in use, having been approved two weeks before my accident. I was

the first person ever to be rescued using this program. If I was hurt two weeks earlier, I would have most likely died.

10. Providentially, there was an ER doctor on the scene vacationing from California. He also just happened to specialize in these types of surf accidents.

For some reason God intervened on my behalf. It is obvious that my time on earth was not yet up.

After being stabilized, the major concern the medical staff had was if I would ever get full use of my hands again. I was told that I *would* walk again (though they did not know how well), but my hands were a more serious problem due to the nerve damage. All I can remember is that my thumbs felt like they were on fire. After a few days I could barely move my fingers. My grip test was virtually zero. My hands were so weak that I couldn't even lift a piece of Kleenex with my thumb and index finger. I couldn't hold a pencil, button a shirt, brush my teeth or even shave. A good friend of mine told me later that when he called the hospital to see how I was doing, he was told that I was lucky to be alive, but that I would most likely never regain the use of my hands.

I remember my occupational therapist, who became a wonderful friend, gently breaking the news to me that due to the extent of the nerve damage, I might not have full use of my fingers again. I asked her if I would possibly have at least one usable finger on each hand. She said, "Yes, there is a strong possibility you will have the use of a finger or two." To which I replied gratefully, "Great, I only need two fingers as I can only type with two!" I was happy to be alive. I knew in my heart of hearts that I was a lot better off than at that beach. Though I was swollen and dealing with burning pain in my hands, I was breathing fairly normally and slowly regaining some feeling in my arms and legs. I had such a fullness of joy and a renewed love of life that I felt like a new man. Though our sabbatical had been sabotaged by the accident, I was not upset. In fact, I believe that what I was undergoing brought more restoration to my soul than any three-month sabbatical could have ever produced.

That evening, my mother called to check on me. She asked me how I was doing and wondered aloud if I was upset or angry with God for what had happened. She figured that it would only be normal for me to be bitter. After all, it had been a very rough year, and now here I was, lying in the hospital, still not completely understanding the full physical repercussions of my injury. She knew that I was a very active person and soon would have to go back home, in a wheelchair, not knowing if I could ever function like I used to. She also knew that my family's trip of a lifetime was now over. For us, there was no more sabbatical to look forward to—just a bumpy and slow road to rehabilitation.

However, my upbeat response surprised her and many others who called. I was in extremely high spirits as I spoke to many concerned friends on the phone. Many expected that I would be sad and bitter. From their perspective, this seemed to be a logical response. However, I surprised them all by how happy I was. There was no bitterness. How could I be upset? I was alive! But I appreciate why they had such a hard time understanding my joy of life. The answer was quite simple—none of them had ever gone through this type of experience. How could they fathom how impossible it was for me to get upset when I was just so thankful to be alive?

Not only was I alive—I was getting stronger. My swollen body was slowly returning to form. The pain in my hands was under medical control and the countless visits from my physical and occupational therapists were slowly allowing me to have gradual mobility. After a few days, I was actually able to sit up for a very brief time in my bed with the help of the nurses and my mechanical bed. However, walking and using my hands were still impossible. After a week, I improved so quickly to the point that some of the medical staff were calling me "the walking miracle," as I was slowly able to take a few steps while strapped to my physiotherapist. For me, I felt that I had another lease on life. There was no way possible that I could hold on to any bitterness at all.

There was another reason I was not upset. In the midst of my pain, I found God. He was with me in the water. He was with me on the beach and in that hospital. And He had never left my side, gently cradling me the whole time. In fact, He had been with me throughout every tragedy of my life. I had never experienced His close presence like I did while going through the three tragedies. It was as if this accident peeled away the final barriers that I had unknowingly constructed between God and I. My water accident became that final key to opening my awareness to God's active presence in my life. Now, in the weeks of recovery that followed, I was experiencing the restoration of my life from the very Spirit of God who lives inside me. Through each tragedy, God was at work on my soul, purging me of every bit of self-ishness. My near-death experience and the physical weakness that ensued was the final segment of His active grace in cleansing my soul. I was now inhabitable to God my Father. He was now bursting forth from within and filling me with His loving presence.

When I was recovering and doing all I could to get feeling back into my legs and arms, I leaned heavily on this Jesus who knew exactly what I was going through. He knew what it was like to suffer. I received great comfort from Him. I wanted a reminder of the God who inhabits my suffering and helps me through it. Once again, I experienced first-hand that He is not a distant God, but one who chose to suffer so that He could always be with us, even in our lowest moments of pain. It was here that I vowed to buy a crucifix as soon as I was strong enough to get out of the hospital as a reminder of my suffering Saviour. I learned something while I was hunting the jewellery stores—there aren't many crucifixes out there. There were plenty of ornamented crosses in gold, silver, with diamond studs and rhinestones, but few crucifixes.

Why is it so hard to find one? I think I know why. Suffering isn't something people like. We would rather avoid it. Fashionable crosses with diamonds are nice. However, there is nothing nice or fashionable about a cross with a person hanging off it. The cross was never meant to be a fancy piece of jewellery worn by rap artists, Hollywood celebrities or superstar athletes. We have made an instrument of suffering into a fashion statement. We have belittled the cross of Jesus. We don't like the crucifix because it reminds us of the reality of suffering. Yet the crucifix brings all the bloody value of the cross into perspective. It is a beautiful pain that results in salvation.

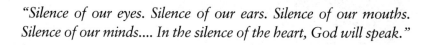

"Silence of our eyes. Silence of our ears. Silence of our mouths. Silence of our minds.... In the silence of the heart, God will speak."

– Author Unknown

THE GOD WHO SPEAKS

◆

CHAPTER FOURTEEN

"What is God telling you?"

These were the very first words I heard as I woke up from a deep sleep after spending my first night in the Maui Memorial Hospital. Through my blurred vision I could slowly make out the figure of a face that was the source of this question. It was my good friend Victor Abuharoon and I was shocked to see him. *What was Vic doing here, leaning against my numb legs, staring inches from my face, asking such a question? After all, he lives miles away in California and here he was, with his family, gathered around my bed in Hawaii, asking me this strange question.* Yet his question sliced deeply into my soul. It was prophetic. This question, though spoken through human means, was actually inspired by God himself. He demanded an answer.

"What is God telling you?"

A strange question to ask someone in my state. There I was, all beat up, paralyzed, barely able to move a muscle, traumatized from a near-fatal accident and this guy has the nerve to ask me this. You would think a concerned friend, upon seeing you for the first time like this with tubes and wires sticking out of your swollen and lame body, would be more compassionate, more diplomatic. You would think that the first words you would hear would be more like, "How are you feeling?" or "Poor you. You must be going through a hard time." Certainly not "What is God telling you?"

This seems to be a harsh question to ask someone who nearly died less than 24 hours earlier. But the truth of the matter is that it was the perfect question for a time like this.

"What is God telling you?" How could I expect any less from Vic? His inquisitive nature could not hold back any pretense of hospital visitation etiquette. He just had to ask this question, and I didn't mind. After all, I knew the man's heart and his family's great love for my family. Vic and his wife Stacy were great friends to us. They had always been there in our times of need and we had done our best to return the favour. We were committed to helping each other grow in our love for God and one another and because of this, we often challenged each other in many matters. Sometimes the truth hurts, but it is still the truth and if we accept it from those we know who love us, we will only grow from such challenges. So here were Vic and Stacy, proving once again their love for us by dropping everything they were doing, pulling their children out of school and flying all the way from California to Hawaii. All of this was done within minutes of hearing about my accident. Both Vic and Stacy knew when they heard the bad news that they had to be with us to help in any way possible. This is what good friends do.

Along with Vic's teachable spirit, he has a tremendous passion for God, a great curiosity of life and a unique ability to cut to the chase, say it like it is and get straight to the core issues of life. This is what makes him a successful businessman and I deeply appreciate his challenging insight and wisdom in my life. We all need Vics in our lives—people who love God and love us enough to ask the tough questions that keep us on track with Him.

"What is God telling you?" It was the right question, given at the right time and it came as no surprise that my friend Vic would be the one to ask it. There was no way Vic was going to allow me to get off the hook on this one. He cared for me too much to let me get away from a true God experience by pampering me with compassionate "gobbledegook." Once again God was speaking through Vic.

I responded to Vic's question by mentally shaking loose the cobwebs that had formed inside my sore and aching head. "Lots. God has been telling me lots of things."

My recovery at Maui Memorial Hospital was the beginning of experiencing God speaking directly to me from the depths of my soul.

God had me where He always wanted me—broken and desperate for Him and Him alone. Now, finally, I was in a state where I could listen to Him. For the next few weeks and during the months of rehab that followed, I was deeply impacted by an intimate encounter with God that is impossible to describe, and it all started when I was left alone for the first time in my room right after I was brought to the hospital from Hamoa Beach.

Lying in my bed in the sacred silence of a typically bland hospital room, I heard God's divine words speak clearly to me and this is what He said: "Colin, you are my son whom I love and with you I am well pleased."

Tears rolled down my cheeks. I was stunned. Words can never explain the strange warmth that I felt throughout my body as I heard God speak my identity to me. Each heavenly word that entered my ears left a loving mark on my soul. At that moment, I didn't just hear that God loved me. I now *felt* His great love for me.

Then it all came back to me. I was reminded of that conversation with my wife only an hour before the accident took place when I confessed that I didn't know who I was. I remembered her puzzled look as she asked me, "How will you be able to know who you are?" "I don't know," I responded, "God will have to take me there."

Well, God had responded to my heart's desire. Little did I know that my confession regarding the longing in my soul to know who I was had become a prophetic prayer. Through a wave God brought me to the only place I could finally hear and experience Him telling me my true identity. In that hospital room I experienced my divine "sonship" for the first time. I understood that God not only loves me but He is also *pleased* with me. My worth in His eyes has nothing to do with what I achieve or how well I perform. Even during my greatest failures He loves me and is well pleased with me. Those freeing words spoken to me by my heavenly Father flooded my soul with incredible peace. The pressure was off. A heavy weight had been lifted from my soul. I was liberated from having to maintain a self-identity built on success. I no longer had to prop up my ego by impressing others with my accomplishments. God loves me and is pleased with me because of one thing—I am His son. Case closed. He has chosen to love me and take pleasure in me. There is nothing I can do to change His mind. God is crazy about me, His son.

This divine encounter with God opened the floodgates where His presence was very real to me. He was speaking so much into my life. Unable to hold a pen, I asked my wife to purchase a small tape recorder, so that I could remember everything He was saying to my heart. When I was eventually able to use my fingers to type, I ended up journalling over 80 pages of thoughts and insights that I believe came directly from God speaking in my soul. I was shown all sorts of things that were present in my life that were hindrances in my own development. God revealed to me things I was never aware of that were deeply rooted in my inner being. I was shown how my active, exterior life, both good and bad, was the direct result of interior motivations, thoughts and feelings that were not necessarily based on God. Most importantly, He brought healing into the depths of my being as He performed life-giving heart surgery on me. This experience of divine intimacy with God is indescribable. There are no human words that can explain what was happening to me. God was with me, speaking to me, and He was closer to me than any person I have ever known in my life.

I was truly blessed through the beautiful disappointments I had encountered. The three trials had broken me to the extent that all I had to cling to for life was God and God alone. These trials had now cleansed my soul of any attachments of misplaced loyalty, and through this purging of suffering, I was brought to the beauty of the indwelling God who inhabits my inner being. I was experiencing God in the deepest place of my soul and I knew why this was such a fresh experience. This deep bond with God was the result of being freed from all the trappings standing between us. I learned that the only avenue to experiencing God is along the road of brokenness. It is so true—you cannot have Christ without the cross.

During my recovery, I was influenced greatly by the historic Christian mystic saint known as John of the Cross. He, along with St. Teresa of Avila, were Carmelite mystics who lived in the 1500s and have written the finest works describing the spiritual practice known as *contemplation*. I was deeply drawn to these Catholic mystics since they were the only experts I knew who could direct my soul in this out of the ordinary spirituality I was experiencing.

Before the accident, I was a driven, type A personality. I was always way out there, serving people, creating ministry projects and running to and fro to make those ministry projects work. Now, all of a sudden, I was bedridden, unable to do anything, forced to stop, think, pray and listen to God. I was fast-tracked, forced by paralysis, to be a contemplative mystic. And the strange thing about all of this was that I was enjoying this new, slower-paced life of silence and stillness. My type A personality was transformed by a wave, causing me to become a contemplative mystic, and it was in the writings of John of the Cross that I received spiritual direction for my new, slower journey with God. John penned the famous quotation, "The dark night of the soul," while in Spain, after he had escaped living in a dampened prison cell in 1577. He used this quote to describe how God works in us when we feel abandoned by His presence. Pain is an occasion that can bring about a "dark night of the soul" experience leaving one's heart excruciatingly broken. Often when people go through extreme suffering, they discover that their old methods of experiencing God no longer work. Spiritual disciplines that used to bring them close to God have become ineffective. In this state of complete spiritual loss, a person's reliance on sacred methods, religious programs and other forms of dependency no longer work. Their ongoing affliction has smashed the old, stale theological box that they have erected to keep God safely at bay. In this state of spiritual loneliness, a person is now teachable to experience the true God. A slow but strong smouldering hunger for God arises in their soul. It becomes unbearable and they realize He is all they want, far above and beyond all other potential loves. This is when one can finally experience God richly. It usually happens through suffering.

It is important to realize that John was a practitioner. He did not just write powerful philosophy or theology regarding suffering and the soul. He was writing what he was *living*—rejection, imprisonment and torture. His writings came from his own experienced truth that you cannot encounter God fully unless you first went through a dark night of the soul. His own dark nights were a time of purging in which his soul was shaken at its core through the extreme trials he faced. These experiences cleansed his soul by emptying him of anything that had control over him.

John believed, as I do now, that for any soul to be filled with God's presence, it has to first undergo a purging that would empty it of any attachment that ruled over a person. These attachments become rival gods if they receive more attention than the one true God. False attachments pose a serious problem in a person's relationship with God simply because anything, even a good thing, that is embraced over and above God is idolatry. The result of idolatry causes a serious breach in the relationship between the idolater and God. The fact of the matter is that God cannot inhabit a soul that has a rival god present.

For the one true God to fill our souls, there must be a destruction of any false gods that are present. Before God can inhabit a soul, it must first become fit for divine habitation. Only empty vessels can be filled. Our souls were made only for God and the Holy of Holies *cannot* and *will not* tolerate any other rivals that inhabit our souls. God is a jealous God and rightfully so. He states that we cannot have any other gods before Him (Exodus 20:3-6).

John of the Cross believed that we can only be partially responsible for purging our souls of any false attachments that stand in the way of our relationship with God. In our own strength, we can only do so much to purge our flesh. The real purging comes when God allows us to suffer. In this way, suffering becomes an incredibly beautiful tragedy of grace—a beautiful disappointment. This is why it is important to not run away from trials and tragedies, but to actually embrace them. This is why we must not ignore suffering. We cannot grow in God if we quit or throw in the towel when tragedies come. Purging can only occur when we detest our tendencies to sweep our pain under the carpet. Only through accepting our suffering circumstances and by walking in them can we be purged from things that block God from inhabiting our souls. For as James says:

> "Consider it a sheer gift, friends, when tests and challenges come at you from all sides. You know that under pressure, your faith-life is forced into the open and shows its true colours. So don't try to get out of anything prematurely. Let it do its work so you become mature and well-developed, not deficient in any way (James 1:2,4, The Message).

I had been tested and challenged by three huge tragedies, and they did their work in me. All the false attachments, those influential voices from the little gods I allowed to control my life, were now being silenced. Finally, I was slowly being enabled to hear the voice of God from the depths of my soul. The question "What is God telling you?" was easy to answer for I finally had ears to hear Him speak.

Whenever someone has enough nerve to ask, "What is God telling you?" the answer should always be, "He is telling me lots of things." Unfortunately, for many of us, we cannot honestly answer this way. This is a shame because God *does* speak to us. The real problem is that we are not listening to Him. We have too many other voices getting our attention and drowning out God's life-giving voice in our soul. These other voices come from various outside pressures to which we have attached ourselves. They have had more of an influence in shaping who we are than God. In essence, we lose out on being the incredible people God created us to be because we prefer the plastic, feel-good voices in our lives that make us feel happy. The problem is that these *happy* voices have no sustenance or value to our soul. When they cease to give us the high we crave, we react like drug addicts and desperately seek another hit—more happy voices to make us feel good. In the pursuit of happiness we lose the source of true, lasting soul satisfaction—experiencing God inhabiting our inner being. Things like our upbringing, cultural and societal expectations, job or ministry demands, media influences, egotistical desires, money, education, family and the like can become false gods that control and shape our being. We end up dancing to the demands of these outside influences instead of following the drumbeat of God. In the onslaught of all of these exterior pressures, we end up losing our true selves as God has created us to be. In time, we no longer even know who we are outside of the titles we possess.

In his wonderful little book, *Let Your Life Speak*,[1] Parker Palmer writes about how we sacrifice our true selves in the forge of exterior pressures:

> "As young people we are surrounded by expectations held by people who are not trying to discern our selfhood, but to fit us into slots. In family, school, religion, society we are trained away from our true selves to images of acceptability and then our original self gets deformed through social pressures and we betray our true selves by fear to gain approval from others.... What a long time it

can take to become the person one always has been. Years, experiences, places. **How often have we worn masks of faces not our own? How much dissolving and shaking of our ego we must endure before we discover our deep identity—the true self!...Our birthright is a gift—live it!**" (emphasis added)

How many of us are truly living the life we were created to be? How many of us truly understand who we are? Most of us are living, walking, breathing deformities of who God truly created us to be.

Ephesians 2:10 states:

"We are God's workmanship, created in Christ Jesus to do good works, which God prepared in advance for us to do." (NIV)

I have to wonder if I am functioning according to Paul's words found in Ephesians. Am I in touch with the true reality of who I am as God's masterpiece, or have I allowed myself to be marred by other outside forces? Do I really know who I am? As Parker Palmer also writes:

"Is the life I am living the same as the life that wants to live inside of me?"

I remember speaking with one of my gifted youth workers while leading a leadership retreat for my staff in beautiful northern Ontario. We were in the middle of a deep conversation regarding the many pressures that leaders face when I asked him, "How much of you has been shaped by God in comparison to how much has been shaped by exterior forces other than God?" His response was revealing. "If you put it that way, then I would have to say that about 90 percent of who I am is the creation of outside influences and only 10 percent is the creation of God."

The two trials I faced began the *process* of purging me of all the attachments, competing voices and exterior influences that were shaping me into being a false self. But it was the *wave* that finished me off. Thank God for that wave. Now I was finally open to God, and He was showing me my true self, who I was, who He created me to be.

The deeper life, which is the most meaningful life available to us, is only accessible in God. To reach God, we must go deep into our souls and wrestle with each and every attachment, outside voice and influence, good and bad, that we have allowed to have control over our lives. This is hard work and will demand sacrifices, but in the end you will find your life. This is what Jesus meant when He said:

> "Anyone who intends to come with me has to let me lead. You're not in the driver's seat—I am. Don't run from suffering; embrace it. Follow me and I'll show you how. Self-help is no help at all. Self-sacrifice is the way, my way, to finding yourself, your true self. What good would it do to get everything you want and lose you, the real you?" (Luke 9:23-25, The Message).

"What is God telling you?" is a question we deeply desire an answer to. In our souls we know that we exist to fellowship with God. We were created for friendship with the divine and the lack of our intimacy with God is disturbing our spirit. "What is God telling you?" points to the desire of all humans—to be friends with God and hear Him speak directly with us. This yearning for God has been wired into us by God Himself. This has been God's original intention for His creation—a strong relationship between humans and Himself. It is still His intention today. However, we have traded in our potential of a relationship with God for flimsy attachments to ego, greed, power, pleasure, things or fear. He wants to be close to us, but we are not listening.

Like Adam and Eve, we try to hide our shame by taking on even more false attachments as fig leaves to hide behind. In the end, we lose out in knowing who we truly have been created to be—our proper identity or real self created by God is now buried underneath an avalanche of false attachments that disfigure us into becoming a false creation. We no longer know who we truly are. Our true need for God has been replaced by our seeking after rival gods and when we trust them over the true God for our identity, purpose and joy, we lose out on living the life we were meant to enjoy. These attachments we seek after for purpose and identity often take the form of our jobs, ministries, reputations, habits, excuses, blame, workaholism, educational degrees, etc. These are just modern-day versions of fig leaves behind which we hide and that cause further division between God and us and between our fellow human beings and ourselves.

God still wants to walk and talk with us on a daily basis. He has even allowed His Son to come and die for our sins that separated us from God. He has done everything at great cost, and through Christ He has made us His children by adopting us into His family. You can't get any closer to God than being His own child! God has done all He can to restore our friendship with Him. He has done all of this for us and yet we still hide.

So, when someone brazenly asks, "What is God telling you?" and we have nothing to say, it is a strong indication that something is wrong and needs to be fixed. Our inability to answer this question bothers us because we intuitively know that we shouldn't be hiding from God. We react so peculiarly to this question of God speaking to us because right down to the foundation of our innermost being we know that our Creator loves us so much but we have settled and relied on false loves.

It is hard to change how we live because our lives have been built on the defective bedrock of false attachments. To allow God to take His rightful place, in our lives means major reconstruction, and this hurts. A purging must take place in our lives and that means pain. The life we are used to living must be destroyed. Things must be re-aligned for this to take place and it means that we can no longer continue living the life we are accustomed to. Our old ways of living, relying on things, titles and appearances for self-worth, must be destroyed and this scares us because it means a total renovation of our being. It means that we have to expose our present state of being and let go of all the attachments that have, like ever-clinging ivy, trapped and hidden our true selves from being manifested. Trials and tribulations can often be God's wonderful way of working transformation in our lives. This is why they can be beautiful disappointments.

When I was injured from my accident, I was instantly connected to God. It was as if the accident purged me of all the false idols present in my soul. For me my idols were my ministry, titles, reputation, skills and giftedness. These were self-made fig leaves on which I had built my self-worth. Now they were of no value to me at all. The importance I had placed in them was now meaningless in light of what I had just been through. With these fig leaves ripped off, I was finally exposed to be a huge phony. With nothing left to hide behind, I was lost, not knowing who I truly was. It was then that I responded to God's calling out to me, "Where are you?" (see Genesis 3:9, NIV).

That wave left me with nothing on which to cling but God alone. Now I was purged, and through my brokenness, I received divine revelation. I now understood how I had seen UrbanPromise as *my* ministry instead of *God's* ministry. I realized that I relied on my titles such as *reverend* or *executive director*, or *a most sought-after speaker*, instead of relying on God and the titles due His name. I cared more about my reputation than God's and trusted in my own skills and abilities over His power. Though I claimed to believe in God, I was acting like a functional atheist. It was only by His grace that I had occasional God encounters during the years of worshipping these idols but now, through the purging caused by these trials, the idols were destroyed and God's glory was present in my life like never before.

I was now free from the imprisonment of the idols of self that I trusted and was now able to experience God bursting forth from the depths of my soul. He had always been present in my life—but I never fully experienced Him because I had been hiding from His presence, unable to see Him, too busy bowing down to the idols of self-confidence. Now at long last, through brokenness, these idols were now destroyed and I was finally free to fully encounter God.

---

[1] Parker Palmer, *Let Your Life Speak: Listening for the Voice of the Vocation.* Jossey-Bass, San Fransisco, California, 1999.

---◆---

"May all your expectations be frustrated, may all your plans be thwarted, may all your desires be withered into nothingness, that you may experience the powerlessness and poverty of a child and sing and dance in the love of God who is Father, Son, and Spirit. And today on planet Earth, may you experience the wonder and beauty of yourself as Abba's child and temple of the Holy Spirit through Jesus Christ our Lord."

– Prayer by Brennan Manning
March 29, 2005

FREEDOM IS FOUND
IN WEAKNESS

◆

CHAPTER FIFTEEN

One evening, my friend Vic paid his daily visit to the hospital. This was part of his usual routine. He would always start the day by taking my family out to breakfast, and then they would all come to the hospital to visit with me. After our time of family visitation, he would spend the rest of the day entertaining everyone with day trips throughout Maui. After dinner, they would all come back and tell me about their day's adventures. Later in the evening, Vic would return to the hospital and visit with me one-on-one. Those late-night visits were sacred times where we would talk with each other, man to man, about the important issues affecting our lives. These special times allowed us to go deep, sharing our faults, weaknesses and desires to improve ourselves as men, husbands and fathers.

We were so transparent with one another because of my tragedy. For me, I had no option but to be *real* with Vic. Having a near-death experience tends to make you vulnerable and open to those you consider your closest friends. As for Vic, I suppose that having nearly lost a close friend also helped him to release the hidden weaknesses and fears that he carried around with him on a day-to-day basis. The truly important things in life had become obvious to us because brushes with death tend to clarify life's priorities. Together, during these hospital visits, we would dig deep into our souls and discover plenty of rubbish that had taken residence inside, garbage that had to be exposed before it could be expelled.

One evening, Vic informed me that he had to leave and return to California. This was to be one of his last late-evening visits. I understood.

157

He had job responsibilities waiting for him back home and they were piling up. I told him how grateful I was that he was the type of friend who would drop everything to support my family and me at such a crucial time of need. While we were talking about his return, he shared with me that he thought he should take my children back with him to Orange County so that Judith and I could focus on my recovery. He made a lot of sense. Knowing our children were being well cared for, we could then concentrate on one thing—my recovery. I began to cry. My children had been through far too much in the past year, and I couldn't bear to let them go. My tears flowed freely and I actually sobbed out loud, thinking about saying goodbye to them. I could tell that Vic was visibly shaken by my reaction, but he could never fully understand what was going on in my mind. I had experienced death and resurrection and had plenty of time to ponder how close I had been to losing my wife and kids. This thought was constantly on my mind during my recovery, and I had vowed to be more available to my family than ever before. But here was my friend now telling me to let my children live with him so my wife and I could focus on my recovery. I was speechless. The emotional state that I was in left me confused and unable to think or even make a decision. *How can I let them go?*

After a few minutes of silence and tears, Vic challenged me with yet another typical well-thought-out, deeply probing question. He asked, "When was the last time you and your wife had time alone?" "Not since my son was born." I'll never forget the look on his face. His entire countenance changed. His face was visibly grieved. It was as if he were experiencing deep pain on my behalf. With a serious tone, he said, "That is so sad. Listen to me, Colin. Me taking the kids back to California with my family could be the best thing for your marriage." Ouch! Those words stung but they were right on the mark. This was not just about me or my children. More importantly, my marriage was at stake. Judith had also been through far too much. She was suffering more than my children or even me. She had experienced the pain of Patrick's loss. She spent days and nights at the Hospital for Sick Children in Toronto, comforting the family of the little boy who drowned. These two horrible circumstances had taken their toll on her as well. But to cap it all off, I can never imagine what it must have been like for her to see my bloated body on the sands of Hamoa Beach. I often wonder what was going on in her heart when she watched me struggling, gurgling and fighting for any drop of air I could suck into my lungs while lying on that beach. *What was she thinking when she saw a crowd circled around my paralyzed body, listening to a doctor yelling commands and saying that things did not look good for me?* All this had happened around her, and she had the dual role of conveying her love for her husband who might be dying while also comforting her children who were also witnessing the event.

She was the one who had to be strong for C.J. and Victoria after I had been medivacked by helicopter, putting her needs aside as she prepared them for the long drive to the hospital, not knowing what she would see when she arrived. What kind of impact did that long two-hour drive have on her psyche? She had far too much time to think about the bad news awaiting her at the hospital. What a horrible emotional toll this must have had on her.

But there was even more pain, a far deeper pain. Judith was also married to a workaholic who for years had championed his ministry over and above his wife. Part of the work God was performing in my heart during my slow recovery was to show me how, during all of my years in ministry, I took my wife for granted as I responded to everyone else's needs while starving her of her voice. For too many years she had heroically served with me, but ministry consumed me. Yes, she needed me now more then ever. In fact, she deserved this and had been waiting for it for years! This truth was confirmed during my recovery in the hospital. God had already been working on me regarding my busyness and neglect of my marriage. Now He was using Vic's words to consolidate everything He had been saying to my soul. God used Vic's challenge to provide a divine opportunity to bring some healing back into Judith's life.

I didn't know how to respond to Vic. On one hand, I knew he was right. His idea of taking my children back to California made perfect sense. It would be the best thing for my kids, my recovery, my wife and our marriage. Yet I was so fragile that I couldn't think straight. I needed Vic's strength to make the decision for me, so I told him that I trusted his wisdom and I would submit to whatever he thought was the right thing to do. Two days later, I was saying goodbye to my children from my hospital bed as they left to catch a plane with Victor and his family.

It was heartwrenching to see my children leave. They had been through so much and now we were being separated.

I was comforted knowing that they were in the excellent, loving hands of our friends. Yet I knew that I would miss them tremendously. My heart broke as they left, but I soon discovered that Vic was right yet again. This was the best thing for our marriage. Each day I came to love this incredibly beautiful, gracious and strong woman even more. I learned to depend on Judith for everything. I needed her to drive, to help me get dressed, to put toothpaste on my toothbrush, and to set up my walker for me as well as organize all of my pills. Once again, I saw how much of a blessed man I was because of her. In the past, she had patiently put up with my ridiculously busy schedule. Now, God had given me a second chance to treat her as she deserved. God had given her back to me to love, cherish and honour. I could now start over again to be the husband to her that I was supposed to be.

Being dependent on others teaches you many lessons in humility. I was forced to depend on so many people during my Hawaiian experience. Doctors, nurses, therapists, Vic, Judith and many others. It was very humbling, as a man, to depend on others to dress me, comb my hair and help me shower. But there are many lessons to be learned in the school of humility.

One of things God gave me while in Maui was a softer heart for those who are weak. I'll never forget the first night I was released from the hospital. We were on our way to the local Wal-Mart to purchase the myriad of drugs that I needed for my recovery. Painkillers, anti-inflammatory pills and all sorts of other goodies. On the way to the store, Judith stopped at the side of the road to buy some gum. As she left the car, I noticed a dark figure slowly coming out of the shadows towards me. The car was still running and the keys were in the ignition. I became extremely fearful because I knew that this young man could easily carjack me and I was in no condition to thwart his attempts. I had never felt this kind of fear before in my life. I had spent most of my life in some really tough inner-city neighbourhoods and was never scared there, but that night, in my weakened condition, I was anxious and fearful that I would be the victim of a crime. This young man walked closer and closer to my car—and then walked straight on by. Nothing happened. I had lost my independence, my pride, my ability to defend myself. I was weak and frightened. I needed Judith for everything. When she returned to the car she noticed how anxious I was. We chatted about my new fear all the way to Wal-Mart. After she parked the car, we slowly made our way into the store.

I was walking at a snail's pace, depending on my walker each step of the way, and then the same fear I had just experienced a few minutes earlier returned. Here I was, trying to navigate the wide aisles of this huge box store, fearful of all the little children running and busy customers who were briskly moving all around me. *What if one of them knocked me down? What if a child plowed into me and I got re-injured?* Once again I had lost my independence. I couldn't even do something as simple as shopping. I had to get out of that store right away. With Judith's help, I was slowly escorted outside the doors of the Wal-Mart to sit on a nearby bench. While waiting outside, I began to feel great empathy towards senior citizens. Compassion for hurting people often comes to those who have already experienced their pain first-hand. I now know how seniors feel because I experienced their world. A world of dizzying speed, great challenges and the need for dependency on others. God softened my heart for those who are weak.

After we had purchased my drugs, we drove to the Roselani Place, a seniors' residence closely associated with Maui Memorial Hospital, where I was to continue my rehab. As we entered the building, I felt a sense of security. The hallways were wide, the elevators were wheelchair and walker friendly. The pace was slow and every few feet there was a button along the walls to press for help in case of medical emergency. We were shown to our little apartment, and when we entered, we sat on the bed and cried. They were strange tears—tears of relief. Finally, I was safe and secure and the stress of Wal-Mart was behind me. I believe Judith cried because of *my* tears. Until now, she had only seen me cry a couple of times, but now her broken-down husband had been transformed into an emotional being.

This was a transformation for the better, but it was still so new to her that she didn't know what to think. So she wept with me. As we cried together, we soon began to laugh. Life has its share of comedy. While giggling uncontrollably, Judith said, "Look at us. We are living in a seniors' home instead of enjoying our trip of a lifetime, and we are still young." Then it hit me. The empathy in my heart that God was giving me towards the weak, and specifically to seniors, was being finalized by having us live here. Here we were, sleeping in separate rooms, eating our meals with other seniors and generally living the life of the aged while still being fairly young. I was truly learning to live a life of weakness. A life of dependence. A life of *freedom.*

You learn many lessons when you are weak and humble, and the most important is that you need to trust God for every detail of your life. Jesus' words: "apart from me you can do nothing" (John 15:5, NIV) are not confined to those of us who are paralyzed and fully dependent on others for survival. They are also written to the so-called strong, healthy, independent folks who think they have all they need, when in reality they have nothing and can do nothing without Jesus.

"Apart from me you can *do nothing.*" How can you do nothing? Yet many of us waste lots of time doing lots of nothing. I began to question how much of my time and busyness over the years was just a pile of nothing. I realized just what doing nothing involved. I saw that the endless activity I performed to prop up my ego really was a load of nothing. I had lived for me and not God. That is doing nothing, and I did a lot of damage by doing so much nothing. In my delusional belief in my so-called independence, I acted like I didn't need God for anything. I had all I needed in *me*, and herein lies the problem. Once your ego is propped up by your own abilities, then you must work hard to keep it elevated. This brings about a life enslaved by performance-based living. This lifestyle produces workaholism and neglect of what is truly important in life. Your own soul suffers. Your friendships and family get neglected and pay a heavy price.

God revealed this to me in my weakness, and in my weakened state of dependence on all sorts of people, I was able to see clearly that my old, independent, "I don't need anyone to help me" self was a self built on nothing. I could no longer ignore my soul, my wife, my family and my friends. I needed them. But more importantly, I needed to depend on Jesus every step of the way. I had now entered a new way of living.

By being forced to be humble and broken, I learned the *freedom* of dependence. The tension I suffered from living for my ego was released. The pressure of performance was gone. I was finally free. In my weakness, I encountered God like never before. Living by dependence on Jesus freed me from the enslavement of independence I falsely thought I had, a false autonomy that was really a prison of my ego. I now understand *exactly* what Paul was talking about when he wrote about God's strength given to us when we are weak:

"He said to me, 'My grace is sufficient for you, for my power is made perfect in weakness.' Therefore I will boast all the more gladly about my weaknesses, so that Christ's power may rest on me. That is why, for Christ's sake, I delight in weaknesses, in insults, in hardships, in persecutions, in difficulties. For when I am weak, then I am strong." (2 Corinthians 12:9,10, NIV)

Weakness causes your soul to cry out to God for support. Ego shuts the door to God. I learned first-hand that when you depend on God *for* everything, you experience God *in* everything. God is in the details of life. He is present at all times. The only reason why we don't experience Him is because we have been blinded by our egos. Our busy lifestyles have desensitized us to His presence. I once was blind—but now I see! Funny how a wave healed me of blindness.

It was clear to my family, other patients and my doctors that this God of the details was with me throughout my recovery. *Immanuel* (God with us) was present. He is present in our world and active in our lives, and He was in my room at Maui Memorial Hospital. Many spiritual conversations took place in that room, wonderful, meaningful, natural conversations about God's active and loving presence in our lives. Nurses, therapists and patients, along with our family, were all impacted by the natural essence of God's pervasive peace present in that room. When people entered my room, they could not help but share their heart struggles and past pains as God performed better heart surgery than any doctor at that fine hospital.

As time went by, God's presence was clearer to me in the many divine moments Judith and I experienced. With my ego now out of the way and my brokenness making me whole, God was revealing Himself to me in a rich new way. It was as if He wanted to reinforce the truth that I was learning—that He was and would continue to be a constant presence in my life. He was teaching me that He is the God of the present, the God who identifies Himself as "I Am." In Exodus 3:13,14, we read:

"Moses said to God, 'Suppose I go to the Israelites and say to them, "The God of your fathers has sent me to you," and they ask me, "What is his name?" Then what shall I tell them?' God said to Moses, 'I Am who I Am. This is what you are to say to the Israelites: "I Am has sent me to you."'" (NIV)

God uses these words—*I Am*—to describe who He is, and in so doing conveys His eternal presence as being the God who encompasses all of history—past, present and future. I receive great comfort in this name for God, simply because it tells me that He is actively present in my life at all times. He has always been with me. He is always present with me now, and He will always be with me in the future for all eternity. When I need Him, He says, "*I Am* here." When I pray, He says, "*I Am* present." When I need His strength throughout the day, He says to me, "Here *I Am*." He is present. He is "I Am." By being forced to slow down, I was able to open my soul to encounter His glorious presence in my life. He had always been present in my life, but now, with the absence of busyness blinding me from His presence, I encountered Him like never before. Through my suffering, my beautiful disappointments had brought me to God. He had always been with me, but now that He had my attention, He was truly proving His love by showing His constant divine presence in my life. He really is the God of the details.

God revealed himself in many ways to me in Hawaii. He still does. There were many intimate revelations that I experienced in my hospital bed where I was reduced to tears from both hearing and experiencing His love in the depths of my soul. He took me back to both my childhood memories and current strivings, showing me things that I had to deal with regarding my soul's greatest needs. I encountered Him each day, enjoying my life in the hospital as family visited me, friends called to speak with me, and my new friends—the doctors, nurses, therapists and fellow patients—spent time with me. I also basked in the presence of God for many hours as I had time to just be still and enjoy His presence with me through reading the Bible or just listening to Him in the silence of my heart.

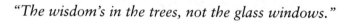

"The wisdom's in the trees, not the glass windows."

– "Breakdown" by Jack Johnson.
From the album *In Between Dreams*,
Jack Johnson, Bush Fire Records,
Universal Music, 2005

WHAT ARE WE GOING TO DO TOGETHER TODAY?

◆

CHAPTER SIXTEEN

As mentioned earlier, when I was strong enough to leave the hospital, Judith and I were sent to a seniors' residence for further recuperation and off-site therapy. Roselani Place was built through the kind donations of a Maui ice cream company and was the perfect place for me to recover. It was built for people who had been slowed down due to physical disabilities. The entrance to the building had a ramp, the nurses were friendly and the hallways were wide. Perfect for slow people like me who needed the assistance of a walker to get around. Needless to say, the seniors were very happy to have us as their guests and we spent many good times together, sharing our meals with some wonderful people. People with names, families, stories and memories. Life was slow in this place and it allowed much time for reflection.

One morning, right after breakfast while I was slowly making my way back to my apartment, leaning on my walker with each step, I thought, *Okay Colin, what are you going to do today?* Then I began to laugh. I believe I heard the Lord chuckling with me and saying, in His gentle, still, quiet voice, *Colin, you can't do a thing. Look at you. You can't even walk by your own strength or even get dressed without help.* I quickly replied, *You are right, Lord. Forgive me. I am sorry. What I should have said is What are we going to do **together** today?* This was the beginning of a new revelation for my life. I could no longer see myself doing things by my own strength.

Now, every morning when I wake up, I ask God, *What are we going to do together today?* Little by little, I am beginning to understand how to live a "together today" life with God. It has been a very slow process of learning how to live a life surrendering my inflated pride and dependence on self and trusting God for everything. However, I have discovered it is the only way to live—in total dependence on Him. Now, with my "What are we going to do together today?" prayer I am aware and open to the God whose presence is with me in everything I do. With this new awareness, I experience God walking with me in my daily routines, and I can see that my frequent life surprises take me into new adventures with Him every day. I am discovering that life is best experienced through trust and dependence on God in every detail of life. In Acts 17:28 we read:

"For in him [God] we live and move and have our being." (NIV)

By praying the "What are we going to do together today?" prayer of dependence on God, something mystical happens. Our eyes open up and we are able to experience the very presence of God all around us. After all "we live and move and have our being" in God, and you can't get any closer than that.

When I think back to those days when I was out of the hospital and involved in my daily rehabilitation in Maui, a few incidents come to mind in which this always-present God revealed Himself to us in very clear ways. I'll never forget the day I finally left the hospital for Roselani Place. I was now improving enough to become an outpatient, where I would return daily to the hospital for rehabilitation exercises. As Judith packed my things, we said our final goodbyes. One of the social workers, with whom we had become very close during my recovery, handed me an envelope and told me to look inside. I opened it and pulled out two slips of paper. The first was a certificate for a three-night stay at the beautiful Ka'anapali Beach Hotel. Tears began to well up in my eyes. This was my dream—to be able to spend a few days on a Hawaiian beach before returning home. Choking back my tears, I pulled out the second slip of paper.

It was a ticket for two to attend the world famous Old Lahaina Luau. This was the second wish I had while stuck in the hospital—to be able to go to a luau while in Hawaii. My dreams were becoming reality. I looked at Judith, and we both began to cry. Our friend told us that after she had seen my reaction to a recent visit I had with my family, she wanted to surprise us with this gift. During that visit, my family excitedly showed me video clips from their day trip to the beach and their evening at a local luau with their Uncle Victor and Aunt Stacy. She knew how much I wanted to experience these two Hawaiian staples—beach and luau—and decided to give them to us as a gift. She had made plans with the hospital to allow me three extra days of recovery after I was strong enough to leave Roselani Place to stay at a hotel before I was to be flown back to Toronto. It was now official. I had doctor's orders that my wife and I would have to go to the Ka'anapali Beach Hotel and the Old Lahaina Luau. Yes, God is in the details.

I'll never forget the day my wife and I took a few hours away from Roselani Place for my first day trip around part of the island of Maui. I was strong enough to sit on the passenger side of our little rental car and enjoy the beautiful sights as we drove around the island. On this trip we decided to stop off at the Olawahoo General Store for a few treats. After three weeks of being stuck in a hospital it felt great to get outside and feel the warm sunshine on my face. As I slowly made my way from our car to the store I leaned on my reliable walker for support. Inside, I noticed a very cheerful man with a huge ear-to-ear grin sitting behind the cash register. His reaction was unavoidable, as out of the corner of my eye I could tell that he was staring at my broken body. He studied my unsteady steps while I staggered around his store to scoop up a chocolate bar and a pack of gum. As I shuffled my way to the cash register, he asked me how I got hurt. His voice was light, gentle and inquisitive. I shared my story with him, and when I was finished, he said to me, "Bradda, God is looking out for you." I chuckled and thought, *If he only knew the truth of his words.*

Then I replied, "Tell me about it." He stared through my eyes, right into my soul. With a newness of conviction in his voice, he exclaimed out loud, "Bradda, I am serious! God is looking out for you!" I felt as if God were speaking through him, confirming His activity in my life. I felt a strange warmth in my heart and had to ask him if he was a Christian. He replied that he was. We began to talk more deeply and I said, "I have run into quite a few Christians on Maui. Are there many on this island?" "No," he replied, "there are not many Christians on Maui. Most of the people here are into the old ways and worship nature, but God is doing a revival here in Maui."

I politely agreed. "You are so right. God is doing something because I am running into lots of Christians here." Then he said something that I will never forget. With a sparkle in his eyes and joy on his face he told me, "Bradda, you know why you here, ah? For revival. God is bringing revival to Maui because He is bringing revival to *your life*. This is about *your* revival." Then he shook his head, wagged his finger in the air and yelled, "Whaaaaa!" I was stunned. His words had a direct hit on my heart. My trip to Maui *was* about reviving my soul. God was breathing new life into me, and I knew that these words from a strange, obscure store clerk were God's very words to me. They had spiritual power. It is amazing how God speaks.

Finally the day came when my physical and occupational therapists gave me the green light to leave Rosalani Place. I was allowed to miss a few days of therapy so I could enjoy a long awaited break at the Ka'anapali Beach Hotel. Now Judith and I could actually have a mini–vacation and enjoy the gift our social worker had gave us.

It was our first evening at this beautiful hotel and we were excited and exhausted all at the same time. We stretched out on our bed, enjoying the chance to talk and relax as the moonlight streamed into our bedroom through the sliding doors that led to our balcony view of the Pacific. This was the first time in weeks that we had our own room to ourselves since we were separated by my hospital stay and then we had separate rooms at the seniors' residence. While relaxing I flippantly told Judith my dream of lying on the beach, under one of the cabanas, with a book in my hand and the sound of the crashing waves nearby.

The only problem was that the rental for these cabanas was very pricey, too pricey for our limited budget. In fact, the restaurants were also too expensive. We were tight on cash and to make matters worse, our insurance agency was not clear regarding our coverage. After weeks of wrangling with our health insurance provider, we were told that they would not cover the airfare for my family to return to Canada. Things were even more complicated as Judith and I would have to fly to California first so we could get our children and then fly home to Toronto. Money, or lack of it, was a real problem and we did not have a clue how we would be able to get back home. So, in light of this concern, renting a cabana was not just a dream, but an impossibility.

The next morning, we went downstairs to have breakfast. With our money quickly depleting, I carefully chose my meal according to the cheapest price on the menu. While eating, a stranger came to our table and said, "I couldn't help but notice you two." I knew why. I have a very pretty, young-looking wife who, at that time in her life, was stuck with a broken-down, walker-dependent husband. He must have been thinking, *What is an attractive woman like that doing stuck with an old guy like him?* He continued. "I am leaving here earlier than expected and will be catching a plane in a few hours, and I wonder if you could use these as I would hate to see them go to waste." He then handed me an envelope and walked away. I opened the envelope and couldn't believe my eyes. Inside was a booklet of coupons and the first coupon I pulled out was for the free use of a cabana for an entire day! Another wish come true. It was as if this complete stranger had been hiding under our bed the night before and had heard everything I said.

But this story gets better. The rest of the envelope was full of coupons for free buffet breakfasts, lunches and dinners! Every one of our meals was covered for our entire three-day stay! Once again, I choked back my tears and while Judith wept, I said, "God truly is in the details."

God had provided for my rescue from certain death. He was healing my once-paralyzed body. He had given us three days at a beautiful world-class hotel. He had provided us with a luau, a cabana for the day and all of our meals. However, we had no money to purchase plane tickets for California to pick up our kids and then fly back home. This was another unexpected expense that we had no chance of meeting. What were we to do? Our only option was to pray to the God of details.

Once again, He did not let us down. During our second day at the hotel, we received a phone call from one of our UrbanPromise board members. Both he and his wife were very committed to our cause and had become good friends to us over the years. They were in constant contact with us while I was recovering in Hawaii. One day, while talking with them over the phone, I was asked to provide them with the hotel's fax number. They were faxing me plane tickets for us to fly to California so we could get our children, then also faxing me four more tickets for my whole family to return to Toronto from Los Angeles. When I received the fax, the tickets were for first class!

All these stories of God's active presence in our lives may seem so foreign to many. Some of you may be thinking, *These are really neat stories, but they don't apply to me. How can I experience God like you did?* Some may be thinking, *Why is it that God often feels so far away? Why do I go through periods of spiritual dryness where God seems to be absent from my life?* Yet standing strong against the claim that God is not involved in our lives is Acts 17:28:

"In him (God) we live and move and have our being." (NIV)

God is always present. He has not moved or abandoned us. So why are there times we feel that He is not here with us?

I remember a funny story about a school of fish that were on a desperate mission to find water. All their lives they had heard of the life-giving blessings of water, so they dedicated themselves to find it. The search consumed their thoughts, actions and entire lives. They tried all sorts of things and did all kinds of activities but could never find it. Some even took on religious traditions, hoping that this would help them experience water. They talked about water, read about water, sang songs about water and even heard great teachers speak on water, but none of them ever felt that they had experienced water.

The point of this story is simple. These fish were so busy seeking water in things, activities and traditions that they never slowed down enough to stop and think about what they were swimming in. All along, the water was there for them to experience. It was giving them life. They "lived and moved and had their being" in water! They were always in its presence—after all, they were fish! But they never experienced it.

Sometimes I feel like those fish. Busy, swimming around, trying to make sense of life, seeking purpose and meaning in what I do or in exteriors—my job, ministry, friends, activities, even religion. We don't realize that our souls hunger for God, so we try to fulfill this hunger with things, work and play. But we are all searching for Him in the wrong places. We wonder where He is, while all along His presence is everywhere. In the midst of all of our busyness of searching, Jesus speaks:

"If anyone is thirsty, let him come to me and drink. Whoever believes in me, as the Scripture has said, streams of living water will flow from within him." (John 7:37,38, NIV)

God is here, always with us. We are in His very presence. It is up to us to cut through all of the loud voices, influences and activities that crowd Him out. This is why the "what are we going to do together, today" prayer is so important. It opens up our souls to the very presence of God in our lives.

Sometimes we need help to recognize God's presence in our lives. Our busy lifestyles can often crowd God out so strongly that we cannot ever, in our own power, experience God. This is why God allows trials to enter. Life's disappointments can often wake us up to our need for God and put an end to our vertigo of busyness. These are the beautiful disappointments that God uses to purge us from all of our busy distractions and wake us up to His presence. This is what happened to me. In the days, weeks and months following the accident, I began to experience this wonderful God who is always all around me.

People often ask me how I am feeling. They have a genuine concern for me, especially in light of all the tragedies I have gone through, one after another. They also are worried for my physical well-being as they see me stumble at times while walking or struggling to run. It is obvious that I have definitely slowed down and they can't help but wonder what my future will be like. I also wonder what the future will bring. My neurosurgeon has said no to surgery for the time being, but he *is* concerned about the scar tissue growing on my spinal cord. This could be a problem in the future. However, when people ask me how I feel, I can't help but tell them that this accident has been the best thing to ever happen to me. I wouldn't trade it for anything in the world.

My positive and enthusiastic response usually catches people off guard. They do not understand how I can be so positively excited by my trials. They wonder, often out loud, how a person can talk about three horrible trials as a positive experience. Some jokingly call me "Job" (named after the biblical Job, who faced so many tragedies). However, it is one of those things that, unless you have gone through it yourself, you will never fully understand. Having a near-death experience when you could have easily lost everything near and dear to you makes you look at life very differently. You no longer take things for granted. Now, whenever I see my wife, I realize how beautiful she really is. When I hear my children laugh, I soak it all in as the most blessed man in the world.

God, family and people have taken their rightful places in my life and it is all so wonderful.

It's like being at death's door and having the opportunity to walk away for a second chance. It changes your old black-and-white world into a brand new one in high-definition, living-out-loud colour. Life is so much more vibrant and exciting. My tragedies have opened my soul to God in new and deepening ways. The physical setbacks I experienced, and continue to deal with, have caused me no other option but to positively embrace my circumstances. My slow recovery has forced me to get off the treadmill of busyness and reflect on the kind of life I am living. This forced time out has caused me to encounter and experience God.

Psalm 62:1,2,5,8 states:

"My soul finds rest in God alone; my salvation comes from him. He alone is my rock and my salvation; he is my fortress, I will never be shaken. Find rest, O my soul, in God alone; my hope comes from him. Trust in him at all times, O people; pour out your hearts to him, for God is our refuge." (NIV)

As I began my slow recovery, I felt like I was starting life anew. I was like a toddler, having to re-learn how to walk and use my hands. I also realized that I would be able to start all over again in other aspects of my life. God was allowing me the opportunity to wipe the slate clean. In many ways, the trials I had endured slowly caused me to die to so many selfish and damaging habits. My near-death experience was the lowest I had ever been, yet, it brought me to the highest peak of my existence.

One day, after we had returned from Hawaii, Judith burst into the house from running errands. She had just shared our story with a woman she had met at the bank. Apparently upon hearing our story, this woman spoke prophetic words to her concerning me. She told Judith, very matter-of-factly, that what I had been through was my true baptism. She said that I had finally died to myself and because of this I was now alive unto God! I could not help but agree with her. I truly felt more alive to Him than ever before.

Shortly after my recovery, I was talking to a man at a fundraising golf tournament we ran for UrbanPromise. He was enthralled with my story and said:

"Colin, you are so blessed to go through this at the halfway mark of your life. Too many people never stop long enough to do a serious review of their lives until they are at the end, dying on their hospital bed. For them, they have many regrets thinking about what they should have done and could have done. They have no time left to make the needed changes in their lives or to take the adventurous risks that can make a difference in their world. But for you, what an amazing opportunity. You have had quality time to reflect on your life and you still have time to make the necessary changes before it is too late!"

He was so right, and it makes you wonder why more people do not take extended time out of their busy schedule, especially at mid-life, to examine where they have come from and where they are going. For me, this time of self-introspection, especially in light of the fact that I should have died, had great significance. I now had another chance, a new opportunity to make changes.

The Bible says that God speaks not in loud or spectacular ways, but in quiet whispers. In 1 Kings 19:11-13, we read how God spoke to Elijah:

"The Lord said, 'Go out and stand on the mountain in the presence of the Lord, for the Lord is about to pass by.' Then a great and powerful wind tore the mountains apart and shattered the rocks before the Lord, but the Lord was not in the wind. After the wind there was an earthquake, but the Lord was not in the earthquake. After the earthquake came a fire, but the Lord was not in the fire. And after the fire came a gentle whisper. When Elijah heard it, he pulled his cloak over his face and went out and stood at the mouth of the cave. Then a voice said to him, 'What are you doing here, Elijah?'" (NIV)

God's words came to Elijah in the form of a gentle whisper. To hear God's whispers you need to stop, be quiet and attentive. For those of us who are too busy or full of pride to do this, we will miss His voice. However, God's love for us abounds. Though He is not the cause of tragedies, He graciously enters them and they become avenues of His grace. In painful circumstances, we are broken and forced to slow down. It is here that we have an opportunity to listen and hear God's whisper to us. His whispers are often heard in the disappointments of life and this causes our disappointments to become beautiful ones.

During my recovery in hospital, I told God that I never wanted to go back to being the same person I was before the accident. With tears in my eyes, I asked Him not to fully heal me if it meant that I would go back to who I was before the accident. I'd prefer to be physically handicapped for the rest of my life, forced to depend on Him for everything, than return to being the healthy, proud, busy, unhearing mute that I once was. To me, this old way of living truly *was* handicapped.

We build up such a reliance on things that are other than God, that beautiful disappointments are the only way we can be freed. To experience God we must be desperate for Him, and brokenness is the key to Godly desperation. It is clear from the example of Scripture that trials can often be doorways to experiencing God in a clear and life-altering manner. You just have to observe the Old Testament history of Israel as an embodiment of this. They constantly experienced a cycle of abandoning God in good times, only to return to Him when a national disaster occured. We also see this cycle happen to individuals in the Old Testament who encountered God in a deeper sense when they were going through trials. Noah experienced God in the flood. Abraham encountered God when he was going to sacrifice his son Isaac. Jacob actually wrestled God, only before he was to encounter his assumedly angry brother who wanted to kill Jacob. Moses walked with God through the trials of the exodus. Shadrach, Meshach and Abednego met God in the fiery furnace in Babylon, Daniel experienced God in a lions' den. And the list goes on. Trials are the doorways to intimacy with God.

There is an important principle to be discovered when people encounter God through trials. God makes an appearance only when we are broken and humbled enough to seek His face. We must be desperate for Him. There is a wonderful place for us to meet God and that is on our face before Him, fearful of living our lives apart from Him. Anything to do with pride, our agenda and our own wisdom must be torn away. We must be left with nothing on our own merit and strength. Recognizing how small we are and how big God is causes us to cry out in humility, knowing our great need for Him. It is when this happens that God moves in and changes lives.

After my accident, I was emotionally, spiritually and physically broken. With my pride in tatters, I turned to God and discovered that there were no longer any obstacles between us. The wall of pride separating me from God had now crumbled into rubble. God and I were now connecting on all frequencies. Isaiah 57:15 had come to fulfillment in me:

> "For this is what the high and lofty One says—he who lives forever, whose name is holy: 'I live in a high and holy place, but also with him who is contrite and lowly in spirit, to revive the spirit of the lowly and to revive the heart of the contrite.'" (NIV)

I was contrite and lowly in spirit and God, who lives inside of me, was now given control to live in me like never before. I was totally broken before Him, and in my broken state I was now free. Free of myself, free of my ideals and free of my pride. These had been obstacles that stood between God and I. Best of all, I was now free to be everything that God created me to be. God and I had now become one, just as Jesus prayed:

> "...Father, just as you are in me and I am in you. May they also be in us... that they may be one as we are one: I in them and you in me." (John 17:21,23, NIV)

So, the good news in the midst of *your* bad news is this—God is speaking to you. Embrace your circumstances and allow them to drive you to your knees. Listen to what God wants to say in the midst of life's storms. Contemplate your circumstances and allow them to humble you into the presence of the King of Kings. Then you, like so many of the saints before us, will encounter the Holy of Holies and your life will never be the same again. Now is the time to stop the search for God and just acknowledge His presence. Slow down, be still and know that He is God (Psalm 46:10). Get away from the busyness and noise of your life and hear His voice in the whisper (1 Kings 19:12). Admit your brokenness and find Him in the midst of your weakness (Isaiah 57:15). Detach yourself from all the things that have taken His place on the throne of your life and discover His presence in your soul (Philippians 3:7-15). God is here and the question is: "What is God telling you?

———————————— ◆ ————————————

"Hello, Hello,
I'm at a place called vertigo.
Lights go down, and all I know
Is that you give me something.
I can feel your love teaching me how.
Your love is teaching me how. How to kneel, kneel."

– "Vertigo" by Bono & The Edge.
From the album *How to Dismantle an*
Atomic Bomb, U2, Island Records, 2004

THE IDOL OF BUSYNESS

◆

CHAPTER SEVENTEEN

I remember my third day at Maui Memorial Hospital when I heard the Lord speak to me, telling me why we do not experience the ever-present God in our lives. He spoke through my specialist, who was checking to see what kind of physical repercussions I was enduring. He had just lifted me up into a sitting position so I could finally be seated upright in my bed. With his hands supporting my weight so I would not fall, I noticed that the entire room began to spin. This spinning was so severe that I began to slowly lean downwards in one direction. When this happened, the specialist pushed me upright again and then I slowly leaned the other direction. I was wobbling, back and forth, unable to sit up under my own strength. The specialist laughed and explained that this was nothing to worry about as I was just experiencing a severe case of vertigo. He told me that in time, "The vertigo will soon end and everything will be normal." These words tugged at my heart and I instantly replied, "Doctor, for years I have had vertigo, but now, for the very first time in my life my vertigo is gone."

He did not know what to say to me. He was a medical expert and he knew that there was no way the vertigo had left me. Just one look at my frail, wobbly body was proof enough. Noticing his confusion, I went on to describe what I meant by declaring myself vertigo-free. I explained:

"Until my accident, I was living in vertigo due to busyness. But now I have been forced to stop and do nothing but contemplate and pray. This has finally cured me of the vertigo that I had brought into my life from my senseless and never-ending activity. Now, for the first time in my life, my vertigo is gone! I can no longer do anything. Now, in the stillness and quietness of my hospital bed, I have been forced to stop and listen to God. He has cured me of my vertigo and I never want to go back to senseless busyness again. Doctor, I have been cured of vertigo."

Webster's Dictionary describes vertigo:

1 a: *a disordered state in which the individual or the individual's surroundings seem to whirl dizzily* b: *a dizzy confused state of mind.*

When I look at our society today, the best word I can use to describe our lifestyle is *vertigo*. Whether we like it or not, it seems that all of us are far too busy, whirling about in a confusing sea of bewilderment. We are a confused and befuddled, schizophrenically busy society.

With all the advancements in technology that are supposed to make our lives simpler, they have in fact made life even more complex. Instead of taking advantage of the time-saving tools of modern technology, we have simply taken on more work. Technological advances have increased our productivity in record time, allowing us more time to increase our workload. Instead of rest, we have chosen to do even more work and the world applauds us for doing this. Are we out of our minds? Why have we allowed this to happen? What does our worship of busyness tell us about ourselves? How can we blindly allow the tools of technology to control us so much? The answer to these questions is simple—we are in vertigo. Our society has thoughtlessly elevated busyness ahead of rest and we have bought this philosophy hook, line and sinker. Just ask yourself: *Why do I admire exhaustion as a sign of prestige and admiration? Why do I celebrate a full Palm Pilot as an indicator of self-importance?* The answer is obvious—we have based our self-esteem in accordance with how full our week is with appointments. The more things we have to do each day, the more important we feel. We are in vertigo.

Vertigo and busyness feed off each other and are dependent upon one another for their survival. This never-ending circle of confusion starts with being too busy. Intense busyness stops us from taking the time out to ask the why questions of life and to think and ponder what is really important in life. When this happens we become deeply involved in thoughtless living and this produces vertigo. In return, vertigo empowers more thoughtless busyness. This is why our society lacks thinkers. We are too busy to go deep in our lives.

My own addiction to busyness became apparent to me in Hawaii. My recovery not only allowed healing to enter me physically, but also forced me to go into withdrawal from my busy lifestyle. All of a sudden, I had only one thing on my agenda: the slow and tedious work of healing and rest. There were no appointments to make (other than my visits with doctors and physiotherapists), no breakfasts, lunches or dinners to attend, no crises to deal with and no conferences to speak at or people to counsel. The only thing on my schedule was time available to recover and enjoy the daily visits from my kids and wife. Paralysis, in this incident, had become an incredible gift to me because it made me stop. I could no longer keep busy because I didn't have the physical capacity to do anything. I was in forced withdrawal. All I could do was take up time and think through my life. It was in this state of forced contemplation that I discovered how much of an addict I was to busyness. I also realized that most of us are also busyness addicts.

Our society seems to revere and even encourage our need to be busy. It is an addiction. This is why we cannot sit still for five minutes without turning the radio on, reaching out to read a newspaper or occupying our mind with our "To Do" list of things that must get done right away. If we sit in silence for five minutes, it seems like an eternity to us. Five minutes of nothingness produces the physiological symptoms of someone on withdrawal—we sweat, get anxious and start to shake! These are very real symptomatic signs of drug withdrawal!

And, like all good addicts who desperately need a fix to feed our addiction, we have embraced our drug of choice (in our case it is busyness) as a healthy lifestyle choice! It seems that the more busy one is the more important he or she is meant to feel. Packed schedules are a goal to shoot for and our day planners have become a shiny gold medal of achievement that proudly display our importance. We have actually justified our addiction to being busy. Why else do we feel that strange drug-like induced adrenaline rush of pride when we write another appointment into our Palm device? Today we get our fix of busyness by having cell phones so that we can talk to someone, anyone, anywhere we go, usually about nothing. Why is it that we cannot go anywhere, even out for a relaxing walk, without a cell phone attached to our belt? Is there anything more ridiculous then seeing someone golfing with a cell phone strapped to his or her waist?—a sure sign of addiction. We also have

"PDAs," personal digital assistants, small computer devices that fit in the palm of our hands that allow us to access our e-mail anywhere we go so we can occupy more of our time reading and writing messages to people we deem important. These PDAs have become so addictive that the successful PDA known as the "BlackBerry" is jokingly referred to as the "Crackberry" for its addictive effect on many of its users who cannot leave home without it attached to their belt clip. It is not uncommon to see these addicts using this device everywhere they go, even when on vacations, in movie theatres or driving their vehicles! These small portable devices, alongside of laptop computers, allow us to bring our work everywhere we travel so we can engage in even more activity at home, on vacation and even during our children's sporting activities.

I have actually seen fathers take their children to their soccer games, then do work on their laptops while the game takes place. People often say, "Life is busy," yet I wonder how much of our busyness is the product of our own creation to feed our addiction. Yet, in the midst of our busy 21st-century schedules, God says:

"Be still, and know that I am God." (Psalm 46:10, NIV)

Perhaps we really don't know God because we can't stand still for more then ten seconds at a time. Could busyness now be the idol of our day, controlling our lives? Could it be taking the place of God? Are we giving our time, our minds, our hearts, our allegiance to something else other than God?

Since my recovery, I have been able to see things in a different light. This slow living that I have been forced to embrace allows me the time to gain wisdom. I love what Proverbs 13:20 says:

"He who walks with the wise grows wise...." (Proverbs 13:20, NIV)

Do you notice something about this verse? It states that if you want to grow in wisdom, you first must *walk* with the wise. It doesn't say for us to *run*. Wise people are not rushing through life. They are *walking*. Wisdom is not found in the hustle and bustle of life. It is found in slowing down. How different this is for so many of us. We rush to and fro, here and there. This is not the case with the wise, they walk! Wise people have found an incredible truth—you can only grow by being slow! Wisdom is not in the hustle and bustle of life. Wisdom is found in slowness. So, if you want to be wise you have to stop running and slow down in order to catch up with the wise.

Busyness is society's addiction, and it is killing us. We have to make a choice—slow down and live or else keep running and die. This truth became very real to me when I was coming back from a wonderful few days at an urban ministry conference held in the United States after my accident. It was a wonderful time of encouragement, sharing ideas and dreaming strategies of how we can better impact our cities. However, I became disturbed by the conversations I had with my fellow urban workers. I noticed that the majority of them were virtually burned out and they didn't even know it. Some were classic cases as they shared how going to work each day was a real chore. It was obvious that they had lost any form of delight or joy in what they did. Others were not as obvious until I tried to engage them in deeper conversations regarding non-work issues. When I brought up subjects not connected to their jobs, they had nothing to say. They had nothing of significance to share regarding life issues outside of their busy work schedules. Their identities were so wrapped up in what they did that they really did not know who they were.

This is what happens to those of us who get addicted to busyness. Just like any drug addict, we lose our true personhood to the intoxicating powers of the drug. Like a true addict, these honourable people were sick in busyness and they didn't know it. They were in denial. Their "helter-skelter" lifestyle had kept them so busy that they could not get off the speeding train that their life had become. They couldn't put the brakes on their demanding lifestyle to really think through why they had bought a ticket for the train ride in the first place. They were now out-of-control train wrecks just waiting to happen! Many of them had health and emotional issues to deal with. Others had suffered divorce. Many others were in the throes of serious marriage problems where they had lost any semblance of relationship with their wife and children. Their busy lifestyle was not only having a negative effect on their own personal well-being, but also on the lives of those who were closest to them—their families.

Though I felt sad about my friends at this conference, my time with them helped me realize how effective my drying-out period in the hospital had been for me. I was now acutely aware of those who were just like I used to be. These were the same people I met year after year, and never in my time with them did I ever think there was something wrong with their busy lifestyle. How could I know any better, for I was one of them and I thought that this was the norm. Like any group of co-dependent drug addicts, we were encouraging each other's habit and reinforcing each other's life of denial.

However, by God's grace an intervention took place in my life with that wave. I was stopped in my tracks and forced to do nothing. I was sent to the hospital like an addict being sent off to rehab in order to dry up. I realized that busyness is an addictive drug and its consequences, when abused, are just as devastating.

When the conference was over I had to take a plane back home. My flight was delayed for two hours and I looked forward to a time to relax, think and pray. While waiting in the busy Chicago airport, I observed how addicted our society truly is to busyness. To me it was a bizarre experience. I just sat in my chair relaxing and enjoying the extra time I now had to contemplate the conference I had attended and journal some thoughts. While I was doing this, everything around me seemed to be on high speed. I felt my life was in slow motion but all around me was busyness. Some people were giving the flight director a hard time because of the delay. They were irate, red faced and stressed out. Those who were not assailing the ticket counter were occupied. Busy people were everywhere engaged in anything they could get their hands on that would prevent them from having to sit alone for five minutes. They were tuned out and tuned into their MP3 players or working hard on their laptops. Many were chatting on their cell phones. More were reading a book, a magazine or a newspaper.

No one sat there peacefully relaxing, while enjoying the gift of time afforded to them with nothing to do. The ironic thing is that I am sure that some of these frantic commuters were looking at me puzzled at the sight they saw. They must have been thinking to themselves; "What is this creepy man doing just sitting there calmly with no MP3 player sticking in his ears, no cell phone, no PDA, laptop or reading material?" I am sure that many of them thought that I had to be strange or deranged! That is how addicted we have all become. So much to do, so little time and woe to the one who has too much time on their hands.

The vertigo of busyness makes us falsely believe that life's purpose can only be found from the outside in. Vertigo preaches that our self-esteem can only be found somewhere outside of ourselves. The honour and respect we seek is some place out there ready to be experienced only through a busy schedule. We falsely assume that the busier we are, the closer our reason for living can be found. So we keep at it, seeking to find our nirvana somewhere outside of ourselves. We get busy seeking meaning in exterior things and when we do not find our reason for life in these exteriors, we then get even busier trying to find it somewhere else out there, in different things. The result of all of this is we get lost deeper and deeper into vertigo.

I was like this. If there ever was a classic case of vertigo I was it. I was a pastor for nineteen years, always on call and always available even at the expense of my family. I chalked up the hours and even grew my ministry into more and more responsibilities by founding UrbanPromise Toronto. I felt that this ministry was my baby, and I wanted it to grow big.

Soon my entire identity was wrapped up in the ministry, and the bigger the successes the ministry had, the greater status I received. This led to a bigger reputation, an increase in speaking engagements and larger responsibilities. With all of these big accomplishments came a bigger ego, and along with all of these so-called successes, the deeper I fell into vertigo. I thought I was climbing the ladder of success, but really I was climbing the ladder of vertigo. In eight years, the ministry grew both in size and in funding demands. To meet both, I had to work even harder. The more hours I put in, the more money poured in. This led to an increase in our ministry programming, our staffing and work for me to do. I fell deeper and deeper into confusing, senseless busyness. I had to do more work. So work I did, and I worked hard. I was thickly entrenched in vertigo, totally in denial and unaware of the true mess I was in. Thank God for my beautiful disappointment that came in the form of a wave.

Busyness prevents us from true self-discovery. It keeps us engaged in other things so that we cannot really know who we truly are, and because of this, we are unable to deal with the deeper-seated issues present in our souls. Busyness is the enemy of our souls, yet God tells us to slow down and "Be still before the Lord and wait patiently for Him..." (Psalm 37:7, NIV).

---◆---

"Don't waste your energy striving for perishable food like that. Work for the food that sticks with you, food that nourishes your lasting life, food the Son of Man provides. He and what he does are guaranteed by God the Father to last."

– John 6:27 (The Message)

WHO IS IN CONTROL?

♦

CHAPTER EIGHTEEN

The new slower me loves nature, and I often take advantage of a nearby conservation land just down the street from my office. While walking in this forest oasis, I find my mind relaxing, allowing me time to dig deep into my soul for important times of recollection and restoration. One of my favourite places in this wooded wonderland where I often find my heart leading me is a beautiful pond surrounded by all sorts of trees, bushes and a various assortment of birds. In order to get to this sacred space, I must walk a short distance past a cement bridge that spans a long winding river. Then I saunter past some tennis courts before strolling around a few old buildings used for storage and straight to my pond.

A few years ago, I went out for one of my hikes. When I set out, it was a gorgeous sunny summer day and everything seemed so perfect. However, while on my trek, I was stunned to see that the bridge I often enjoyed standing upon was totally washed away. All that was left were a few tumbled cement blocks on each side of the riverbank. As I made my way past the tennis courts, I could see they were buried under two feet of mud. The fences that once surrounded the courts were piled in a tangled mass of iron and steel. Just past this mass of silt and devastation, I came across those old storage buildings but they were now in rubble. Obliterated bridges, destroyed tennis courts and ruined buildings. *What happened here?*

I returned to my office and told some of my staff what I had seen. Their response amazed me. Apparently, just a few days earlier, a flash flood had swept through the valley and left its destructive mark upon everything in its path. I was unaware of this news as I had been out of the country when it happened. With great curiosity, I decided to return to my hallowed pond for another look. I wanted to learn more about the destructive powers of nature that shaped this valley. When I returned, I immediately began to sift through the rubble and noticed something very interesting. The only things that survived the flood were the structures that were built upon a solid foundation. The seemingly strong cement bridge that had once majestically spanned the river and was now left in tatters had been built upon the sandy banks of the river. The tennis court fences, which had once towered around the tennis courts but were now scrap metal, had rested on a foundation of crumbling cement. The old wooden storage sheds had no underpinning as they were built on top of the earth. These structures were no match for the flood. But the trees that were rooted deep into the earth still stood strong. Their roots dug deep into the soil, gripping steadfastly onto solid rock.

I learned something important that day. As I walked past that mess of a bridge, I began to think about the floods of life that rain down on us all. While tripping over the fallen chain-link fence scattered about the grounds of the abandoned tennis courts, I was forced to examine the true state of my soul. As I picked through the remains of rotten wood that once made up bright, colourful garden sheds, I was left with this haunting question—*When the floods of life pour down on my life, what kind of foundation do I have?*

Then, in the depths of my being, I heard that strong, quiet voice: *Who is in control of **your** life?*

What a great question. It forces us to go deep inside ourselves to examine our life's foundation. It jolts us into reality and helps us understand that whoever and whatever controls us shapes our destiny. It challenges us to examine our souls to see if the controlling power in our lives is built upon a solid and trustworthy foundation. If not, then we are in trouble. What will happen to us when the storms of life blow through our souls? Will we stand strong or will we, like those crumbled structures in my devastated wasteland of a hike, get swept away?

It amazes me that people who actually believe that they are in control of their lives never ask themselves: "Do I really trust my life in my own hands?" When we really think about who *is* in control, we will discover what little power we truly have. Too often we think we are in charge of our life. We manage to deceive ourselves into believing that we have our act together. For most of us, this assumed self-control deceives us into building great confidence. We stand tall, like those chain-link fences that once surrounded the tennis courts. But we are not rooted in a solid foundation. When the floods come, and they will, we will be destroyed.

There are many factors controlling us. They only prove how impossible it is to control our own lives. I have learned that they exert such a powerful, coercive spirit over us and are located in our past, present and future lives. All are very weak foundations.

For some of us, our past controls our present and future. Negative experiences that occurred to us in childhood have shaped us and control our actions even now. Their power over our lives will continue to have an effect on our future unless they are dealt with at their root cause. A good example of this is found in the numerous studies that show that a female who never received the security found in the love of her father is often controlled by an excessive desire to find this love and affection from another male. Many teenaged girls who become pregnant do so in an attempt to find the love of their emotionally absent fathers. Other statistics indicate that a disproportionate number of male criminals doing time in our nation's prisons are from single-parent, mother-led homes. For these prisoners, the anger from the neglect of their father has transcribed into criminal behaviour. These are extreme examples, but we all have to admit that our past has a degree of control over us now in the present. Typical childhood stresses have shaped our self-confidence, social conditioning and general outlook of life.

For others, our present controls us. The current expectations of our bosses, teachers, parents, friends, etc. have inordinate control over what we think, say and do. To this list you can also add the constant presence of the influence of outside forces, such as the media, in shaping how we perceive ourselves and life around us. Because of these present forces, we do not act from the core of our being but, like a chameleon, we change our colours and shapes to fit the expectations of others and the pressures present from the values emitted by our society. We are weak souls indeed, willing victims of the present influences that surround us all.

Many more of us are controlled by the future. Our lives are built around our goals and aspirations to achieve tomorrow's success. We work hard now so we can get the things we want in the years to come. The time we have available for us to enjoy our lives, families and friends in the present is swallowed up by long hours on the job so we can feed our obsessions. The drive to succeed as seen in our eyes, but shaped by our past and present influences, has power over our social, spiritual, physical and emotional needs. This thirst for future accomplishments causes us to live our lives by being controlled by the future. If we are honest, we would have to admit that one or more of these past, present or future forces has control over us. However, we all have to admit that we are all controlled by portions of all three.

Our past experiences, present pressures and future hopes take on various levels of command over our lives. I know many men who are driven by the future goal of success simply because they are trying to prove to the uncaring father of their past that they are worthy of his praise. These men struggle with their own self-esteem in the present, because their father in the past made them feel they could never measure up to their own ideal of success. In turn, their fathers had inordinate expectations heaped upon them because of *their* past experiences with their *own* fathers. And the cycle continues. Past experiences, affecting present actions, influencing future goals. We are like marionettes, our past, present and future join together to pull the strings of our emotions, thoughts, words and actions.

Many of us have survived quite well in our dysfunction. Like a neglected child who has only experienced living in a filthy tenement, we have become used to our out-of-control lives. For us, there has never been an alternative experience. Without another option, we continue living unfulfilled lives without even realizing our needy condition. We think that we are in the driver's seat and that everything is okay until our brakes seize and our steering wheel fails. All of a sudden, we swerve out of control and are hit, head on, by an unmovable object. It then becomes obvious that we really did not have as much control as we thought. The horrible circumstances that led to our accident now reveal our weakness, and we are humbled enough to see how we have been shaped and controlled by the past, present and future.

I now fully understand what little control I have over my life. Though I still make short-term plans for the present and long-term goals for the future, I realize that all of my aspirations and expectations can change in an instant without warning. You tend to learn this lesson well after having lost a young man to murder, a child to drowning and being paralyzed under water. Without my permission, I had been fast-tracked in my journey of learning. I now know that there is only one way to handle the truth of our utter weakness and lack of control of life. We must live a life surrendered to God and His ways.

A year after my sabbatical experience, I had the opportunity to speak to a group of busy youth workers. The theme was boundaries and protecting yourself and your family from being devoured by the pressures of youth work. When my day-and-a-half seminar ended, the host of the conference asked a pastor there to come up and pray over me. I will never forget his prayer. With his hands laid on my bowed-down head and in a booming voice that echoed throughout the auditorium, he prayed:

> "Dear heavenly Father. We thank you for our brother here who has come and shared the important lessons from the many, many life mistakes he has made. He truly is a testimony of failure. We thank you that he has openly shared his weaknesses with all of us. From his mistakes, we are all blessed. And Father we thank you that, spiritually speaking, he has finally graduated kindergarten...."

And he continued to pray like this. As he did, I felt anger build up inside of me—the result of the embarrassment of having this stranger rip into my personal life as he detailed my mistakes, one after another, in front of this group of strangers. There was nothing I could do as this man spoke loudly through a microphone thanking God for how much of a screw up I was. He had heard me share all of my dirt and now was openly rubbing it all back into my face. Worst of all, I had nothing on him to sling back. I was set up with nowhere to run or hide. All I could do was take it all in as he verbally, yet prayerfully, beat me up in front of a room full of people.

I have to admit that those words hurt me deeply. *Finally graduated kindergarten? Who did this joker think he was? Who did he think I was—a spiritual freak?* It really bothered me. My pride was damaged and I felt embarrassed.

However, as he continued to pray, I began to feel better. In fact, by the time he was finished with me and had thoroughly thrashed me spiritually, I felt great and, as he was concluding his prayer, I could not help but join him in agreement with hearty "Amens" and "uh huhs" that arose from deep within my soul. In fact, I believe that I heard God speaking through his prayer, especially when he made that comment about me finally graduating kindergarten. I felt God telling me, excitedly like a very proud parent, that I had grown spiritually through my year of trials and heartache. Graduating kindergarten is a big deal when you are a toddler. And in my faith walk, this is exactly what I am.

Spiritually speaking, I wonder how many of us are still in kindergarten. Kindergarteners tend to get their cues from what other people tell them to do, think, act and say. They live to please others. This sounds like many people and leaders I know, including me. How often we live our lives performing to please others in order to gain little approval stickers from the crowd around us. When this happens, we must ask ourselves: *Who is in control of our lives? How much of our lives are shaped, not from within where God inhabits our souls, but from without by the outside influences and expectations of others?* The answers to these questions will reveal to you if you have graduated kindergarten or not.

I remember when I graduated kindergarten. It was on Hamoa Beach on that fateful November day. Physically I was a grown man, a husband and father, but spiritually I was finally graduating kindergarten. My graduation ceremony started during my conversation with my wife as I shared with her my desire to know who I was. The ceremony ended when I heard God reveal to me my identity in Him while laid out in the hospital room at Maui Memorial.

It is strange that it took this near-death experience for me to come into contact with my soul, but looking back I am grateful for my accident. All I can say is that often the varied waves we go through in life, the many disappointments, trials and tribulations we face, can be divine opportunities to teach us many things about ourselves. More often than not, we need the harsh experiences of life to chip away all the false misconceptions and built-in self-confidence we have on the **outside** to cause us to see who we truly are deep **inside**.

For me, it took a physical wave to literally knock sense into me, forcing me to finally go deep into my soul where I was able to find out who I really was. For others, it can be an illness, layoff, divorce, abandonment or any other traumatic experience that can either destroy us or, if we listen to our souls instead of our losses, open the door to a new and better life. The important things in life fall into place when struggles prevail. Struggles help us graduate simply because all the outside forces that have shaped us and the outer things we have depended on in the past for our little appreciation stickers and rewards no longer work. We are forced to turn within, to where God dwells.

In my case, I was forced to see that my entire identity was wrapped up in what I did for a job. I was totally wrapped up in my ministry. I didn't know who I was simply because I was so busy doing what I thought were very important things. I had falsely believed that who I was was what I did. I had, in essence, stopped being a human *being* because I was so busy being a human *doer*. Thanks to my busy schedule of constant activity, I lost my soul to being a doer. I was everything that others expected from me. I was my charity. I was a speaker, helper, counsellor and visionary—a super reverend. Just a pile of titles and job requirements against which others expected me to measure up. I was a robot controlled not from within where God inhabits my soul, but from the outside where circumstances and people controlled me. Outside forces shaped me and dictated how to think, act and perform. I was the fulfilment of what Erich Fromm observed when he wrote:

"Today we come across an individual who behaves like an automaton, who does not know or understand himself, and the only person that he knows is the person that he is supposed to be, whose meaningless chatter has replaced communicative speech, whose synthetic smile has replaced genuine laughter, and whose sense of dull despair has taken the place of genuine pain. Two statements may be said concerning this individual. One, he suffers from defects of spontaneity and individuality, which may seem incurable. At the same time it may be said of him that he does not differ essentially from millions of the rest of us who walk upon this earth." [1]

I now see that I was like a child trying to please everyone else to get the strokes I craved. I unknowingly was living a kindergarten existence. I lost my *self* in the outside expectations and pressures around me, and it took a toll on my family life and worst of all, on my soul. On the outside, I looked good because my performance was a real showstopper for all those who looked and cheered me on. But on the inside, I was empty, tired, a mess. Thank God for that wave.

As I meet with business and church leaders today, I see this common trait often. They are trapped, like I was, into the performance mode that can so easily control us. They are out of control, like I was. They are my fellow students in the kindergarten of life.

We all struggle to grow up and graduate. This struggle is a battle for control of the pressures of performance-based living. Shortly after I returned from my accident, I had the opportunity to go for lunch with some business friends of mine. These wonderful men own and operate their own successful businesses and are all tremendous supporters of UrbanPromise. I have great respect for them as they have a real desire to use their industry gifting to make our city a better place in which to live. During that lunch, we discussed my experience in Hawaii and I asked them, "What are *your* goals?" They immediately went into performance mode and began sharing their business goals and strategies for the upcoming years.

What was interesting was that they instantly thought that my question was concerned with performance, when the real intent was to listen to their personal life goals. I mistakenly thought that they would be able to clearly define their personal goals as a husband, father and individual. Instead, they went right to their business pursuits and straight to their performance demands. Isn't that the way for most of us? We can more clearly plan and dream up goals for our work over and above what is really important—our soul goals. In fact, many of us don't have a clue where to start when coming up with soul goals.

When I pointed this out, they admitted that they had not given much thought to their personal life goals. Then I said, "You have shared with me how you plan to make your business bigger and more successful, but you haven't counted the cost involved in having a bigger and better company. What kind of toll will your goals for business expansion take on your personal and family lives? The bigger your company gets, the more you will have to feed the beast. The more you have to feed the beast, the more stress, pressures and demands are involved, and the less energy and time you will have for your family and personal lives." I then asked, "Why do you have to be bigger? Who told you that you must always get bigger? You already drive nice cars, have beautiful, large houses and take wonderful vacations each year. Why get bigger? Don't you have enough?" This question blew them out of the water. They nervously stuttered and coughed and then there was an embarrassing silence. They had no answers. Then one of these gentlemen spoke:

"No one has ever challenged us **not** to get bigger. It is just assumed that getting bigger is what you are supposed to do. In the business world there is an unwritten rule—bigger is better."

And that statement proves my point. Who is in control? Who writes the unwritten rules by which we abide? How easily we allow outside expectations to shape our lives and our destinies. If certain things are just something that you are supposed to do and these assumptions are left unchallenged, then who is calling the shots in your life? Is bigger really better? What toll does being big take on our souls, our marriages, our family lives and our futures? Is getting bigger the end goal, the nirvana, of all life?

So many of us are lost in the merciless jungles of the *bigger is better* and *busy is best* mantras. Because of this, so many of us are running around at dizzying speeds, unable to find the time to fulfill our most important task—to take care of our souls. Without slowing down for soul care, we are unable to think through our actions from a divine perspective. In so doing, we allow idolatrous influences to shape our hearts. We lose our true identity by not allowing God, who is the only one with sole proprietorship over us, to shape our souls. The words of Jesus echo throughout eternity:

"What good would it do to get everything you want and lose you, the real you?" (Luke 9:25, The Message)

The battle for control rages between the exterior influences of outside forces, expectations and philosophies versus God, who alone gives true life. Nothing is more precious than the real you inside your soul. Who is in control of *your* life?

This dilemma of the vertigo of busyness and performance-oriented living is not just a business world problem. It is taking its toll on ministry leaders as well. Ironically, many people whom we look to for spiritual guidance are struggling with empty souls themselves. A few years ago, a friend of mine was involved in organizing a conference for Christian youth workers. She was the perfect candidate to be involved in leading this conference since she had many years of experience in youth ministry and was a specialist when it came to counselling youth ministry leaders. This conference had many exceptional speakers, seasoned workshop leaders and a terrific worship band. It was a youth worker's dream to be able to get away for a weekend and soak in the many "how-tos" of youth ministry that permeated this incredible event. However, my friend told me that the highlight of the whole week-end came from an unexpected speaker who also was a contemplative Catholic priest by the name of Henri Nouwen.

Henri Nouwen was a very gifted man who has written extensively in the area of spiritual formation. Though his books do not waste many words or contain many pages, I am glad because whenever I read Nouwen I have to re-read each page as every sentence overflows with insight and wisdom. If I take a highlighter to these books (as I usually do when I read) each word he writes becomes bright yellow. Needless to say, he lived the deep life and his books burst forth with the message that he lived—go deep! Henri Nouwen was not supposed to speak at this conference. His role was to be available to provide spiritual direction to any youth worker who desired his counsel.

However, after meeting countless burnt-out youth workers and experiencing the feverish pace of all the activity that took place at the conference (many sessions and workshops teaching the conference participants to do even more), Nouwen felt compelled to speak. His request to share his thoughts to the participants of the conference was granted by the leadership team as they knew that this humble man must have had a good reason to have such a compulsion to speak. It was only fitting that Nouwen's words to everyone at that conference would be the last words they would hear after a busy weekend of learning the many strategies and best practices of ministry. I wish I had been there that day so that I could quote him accurately. My paraphrased version of what he said does no justice whatsoever to the eloquence and intellect of Henri Nouwen. However, I do believe that the heart of his words are felt and though they lack the Nouwen depth, they still have meaning to those of us in leadership who are very busy doing God's work:

"Dear friends. I must tell you that I am very impressed by you evangelicals. I am impressed by your love for God. I see it when I watch you worship, hear your speakers and listen to every one of you who have come to speak with me. I also am impressed by your love for God's work.

You are very busy serving Him by doing so much for the kingdom of God. It is obvious to me that embedded in each one of you is a very deep passion for God and His work. However, I must tell you that though I am impressed, I am worried, very worried. My anxiety for you is based on my concern for your souls. I am worried about your souls. For in your love for God and your passion for His work you are very busy. **In fact, you are far too busy and your souls have become far too empty!**"

When my friend first shared these words with me I thought they were very interesting and challenging. Yet they did not impact me like they do today. Through the refinement of age and the many experiences and trials I endure, I now feel their heaviness. They are profound. This contemplative Catholic priest's observation of our evangelical soul is now a concern that I too share. I agree with Nouwen, simply because I was a busy pastor caring for everyone else's soul but mine. We have a soul problem because we are far too busy. We as Christians do love God and we are active doing many wonderful things—great kingdom things. We are busy in youth and urban ministries, church planting, counselling, ministry to the poor, ministry in the third world, preaching, teaching, discipleship, outreach, pastoring mega and smaller churches, etc. On top of all of our ministry responsibilities, we also have to deal with our own personal concerns as well as the important privilege of caring for our families.

Unfortunately, for many of us our personal and family lives have taken a pounding simply because we are so busy dealing with everybody else's problems. Our ministry life of doing kingdom things is killing our very souls. Busy, busy, busy, but our souls are empty, hollow, shallow and weak. This dilemma of the empty soul has a strange effect on us. Instead of turning within to God, who alone can fill our soul's needs, we end up doing even more. We ramp up our already busy schedules to even higher degrees of activity to fill the void. We do even more ministry, more work, more hours on the job, etc. We won't slow down because we are afraid to deal with our souls. So we keep active, working hard in business and ministry, dealing with everyone else's problems but our own. For those of us who are Christians, it is a lot easier doing our good works than to examine our own souls. But in the midst of all our good works, something is terribly wrong. We are far too busy and our souls are far too empty.

I have learned that you can only run on an empty soul for so long before something crashes. I have experienced this problem frequently, and my soul and family life have paid the price. But I am not alone. There are many more busy people like me, who have felt or are currently feeling the effects of the empty soul. The real problem is: *How can you be a good husband, wife or parent if you are soulless? How can you have an impact on your community if you are running on empty?*

It takes the God living in you to impact those around you, but if you are not spending time caring for your soul and allowing God the freedom to reign *in you*, then how can you function productively? In fact, if you can't care for your own soul, then how can you care for someone else's soul?

Self-care or soul care rarely becomes a priority in the absence of tragedy. When life is easy and comfy, we tend to get flabby and shallow. We get caught up in the routines of life and go with the ebb and flow of what our society, job and responsibilities dictate. Comfortable is a dangerous place to be.

But then, as strange as this may sound, we are blessed by unexpected trials that come our way. Life begins to get hard, and it is here, in the midst of our struggles, that the blessing is found if we are willing to look for it. Trials tend to grab our attention and make us set our priorities in order. Going through hard times forces us to go deep into our very souls to dig up any form of inner strength we can find.

---

[1] Eric Fromm, *The Same Society,* Routledge, New York, New York, 1998, p. 16.

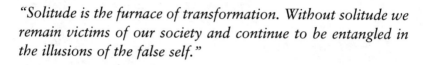

"Solitude is the furnace of transformation. Without solitude we remain victims of our society and continue to be entangled in the illusions of the false self."

– Henri Nouwen

EPILOGUE

---◆---

As I write these final words, I can't help but listen to the noise of the cool November winds blowing just outside my study walls. I watch the squirrels scurry to and fro amidst the waltz of autumn leaves swirling across the dance floor of my backyard. It is hard to believe that three years have passed since I faced those nine months of ordeals. Things are peaceful now, but I am often brought back to those fateful events. Whenever I walk into Patrick's community, I expect to see him slowly walking down the street with four little kids hanging onto each arm and leg. I still have dreams where I am back in the waiting room of the Hospital for Sick Children, sitting next to a grieving family. There are times I am flipping TV channels and come across a scene of a sunny tropical beach. In the back of my mind I drift back to Hawaii where I am at Hamoa Beach, drowning again under the emerald waters of the Pacific.

And of course, I also have the physical repercussions as reminders of my accident. Each time I turn my head, I hear the grinding of loose cartilage ringing inside my neck. When I try to run, I am slowed down considerably by my heavy feet. These are reminders of my weakness declaring to me that I am not God. I have no power over what is happening and will happen in my life. Things just happen. They may be surprises to me, but never to God.

In the corner of my office is a souvenir that I have purposefully set up as a reminder of my need for God. It is my aluminium Guardian model 30755P walker. It was this very piece of medical ingenuity that taught me how to walk again, both physically and spiritually. This walker was God's divine tool allowing me the opportunity to truly walk again, slowly, alertly and dependently on Him for each step I took. Though physically I don't need that walker anymore, I still cling to it spiritually. It reminds me to slow down, be alert to life all around me and trust God for every step I take. This slowness of pace has taught me to become contemplative and cherish the times of silence and solitude where I am enabled to be touched by the ever-present God who has set up residence deep within me.

I enjoy spending sacred time in stillness listening to God's voice within my soul. It is here that He speaks life into my emptiness. However, it doesn't stop here. My sacred time with Him continues with me asking again, *What are we going to do together today?* And in that prayer I lean on Him, like I leaned on my walker for support, guidance and freedom. Then throughout the day, I revel in His continuing presence with me. He reveals Himself in the nature that surrounds me. He speaks to me through the words of those I meet. I am blessed to hear His laughter in the children gathered at one of our after-school programs or at the school where I just dropped off my daughter. He is present in the smile of my wife and in the tears of my children. God is present everywhere speaking life into my soul. All I need to receive His words to me is a listening spirit.

My wife and I recently had the opportunity to return to Maui, and as fate would have it, we were both back at Hamoa Beach on my birthday, three years after the accident occurred. It was a dark, stormy day and the wind was howling at us, blowing a steady windy rain into our faces as we stood hand in hand on the beach staring back into the tumultuous ocean. It was as if Hamoa Beach was angry to see me again, irritably desiring a second chance to take me out. Each loud pounding wave descended menacingly at our feet and I was humbled once again by the strength of the ocean.

I was left speechless as countless flashbacks of "that fateful day" replayed in the theatre of my mind. The beautiful sunshine that greeted us that morning. The joyful anticipation of a great day in the surf. The smiling faces of my children danced before my eyes and their boisterous laughter rang in my ears once again as I envisioned them with their boogie boards in hand. I swear I could hear my son warn me of the present danger he saw in the immensity of the waves. Then I saw myself back in that ocean riding that wave, that big, scary, wonderful wave as it took me down, driving my body headfirst into the ocean floor. In my mind's eye, I was under the water again fighting for my life as my paralyzed body floated amid the torrent of sand and bubbles all around me.

My mind's journey back through time was ended abruptly when I looked at my wife and saw tears streaming down her lovely face. She too was reliving her own horror story of nearly losing her husband on this beach only three years ago. But there was much more going on in the depths of her soul. The return to Hamoa Beach opened the door to the entire journey of the past three years. This painful reunion enabled her to relive both the physical and psychological struggles that we had to overcome as individuals and as a family. The toll of our year of tragedy left its imprint on us, but now we were stronger, wiser and our love for each other as a couple and family had become deeper.

With the waves pounding ominously all around us, we both bent down and scooped up some sand from the beach and placed it in a bottle. This was to be a keepsake of God's faithfulness to us. However, the more I ponder that sandy bottle now sitting on my desk back home, the more I have come to understand that there is a much deeper message hidden among each volcanic black granule of sand stuffed in that bottle. God is using this monument of sand to remind me of how futile my pre-accident life was. The sand cries out that a life built on things other than God is a life that will collapse when storms arise.

"But if you just use my words in Bible studies and don't work them into your life, you are like a stupid carpenter who built his house on the sandy beach. When a storm rolled in and the waves came up, it collapsed like a house of cards." (Matthew 7:26,27, The Message)

Now, thanks to God's wave, His beautiful disappointment, my old life has been torn down, the sandy foundation demolished. I have been restored while I am still being renovated. My new life is now built on the solid rock foundation of hearing the words of Jesus living in me! Now, we are together. God and I, I and God. There is no greater foundation than this.

When we arrived back at our hotel from our return visit to Hamoa Beach, I lay down in my bed, a changed man. My thoughts went back to the days when I was in rehab learning how to walk all over again through the help of the parallel bars that supported my body. I remember leaning on those bars to support my weight as I valiantly struggled to move my body, one small step at a time. I realized that this was a perfect analogy of what was happening in my life. Physically I had to learn how to walk all over again. Now, spiritually I was learning to walk with God. I have a new life. A more mature way of living. Good things come out of beautiful disappointments.

Clutching my sleeping wife in my arms, I smiled, knowing that tomorrow is another adventure with the living God, my friend, my Father and my foundation. I had the best sleep of my life.

"Now I take limitations in stride, and with good cheer, these limitations that cut me down to size—abuse, accidents, opposition, bad breaks. I just let Christ take over! And so the weaker I get, the stronger I become." (2 Corinthians 12:10, The Message)

Join the Community

If you enjoyed the stories and lessons learned in this book, then why not get more involved? We have a section designed specifically for our readers on the UrbanPromise web site. It contains a downloadable discussion guide for personal or small group study.

To learn more about UrbanPromise Toronto and to discover the many opportunities for you to get involved,

log onto:
www.urbanpromise.com

or contact us by phone at:
(416) 516-6121 ext. 21.

Colin McCartney is also available to speak on matters concerning the soul; men's, youth and urban issues; and other topics at corporate, church or other functions.

To book Colin McCartney for one of your functions,

log onto:
www.urbanpromise.com/up-speakers.htm

and complete the online form.

Castle Quay Books

OTHER CASTLE QUAY TITLES INCLUDE:

Walking Towards Hope

The Chicago Healer

Seven Angels for Seven Days

Making Your Dreams Your Destiny

The Way They Should Go

The Defilers

Jesus and Caesar

Jason Has Been Shot!

The Cardboard Shack Beneath the Bridge - **NEW!**

Keep On Standing - **NEW!**

To My Family - **NEW!**

Through Fire & Sea - **NEW!**

One Smooth Stone - **NEW!**

BAYRIDGE BOOKS TITLES:

Counterfeit Code:Answering The Da Vinci Code Heresies

Father to the Fatherless: The Charles Mulli Story

Wars Are Never Enough: The Joao Matwawana Story

More Faithful Than We Think

For more information and to explore the rest of our titles visit
www.castlequaybooks.com